# "SLICK WILLIE"

## Why America Cannot Trust Bill Clinton

### FLOYD G. BROWN

D0042800

Annapolis-Washington Book Publishers, Inc.
Annapolis, Maryland

ISBN: 0-9634397-1-5

Annapolis-Washington Book Publishers, Inc.
P.O. Box 2365
Annapolis, MD 21404

*Cover photograph courtesy of*
*Bettmann Archives*

*Jacket design by*
*Jim Laurier*

# CONTENTS

# Author's Preface

There are two reasons why I wrote this book.

First, the media failed to tell the full truth about Bill Clinton. Perhaps they were fascinated by him. Perhaps many supported him. Whatever their reasons, they simply refused to make him tell the full truth. And they never told the truth about him. About his draft record. About his record as Governor of Arkansas. About taxes and education. And about his conduct as an individual.

Now Bill Clinton sits in the Oval Office. He is leader of the country that heads the free world. The American people should know his record. His use of marijuana. His use of the Arkansas governor's office to help his friends and family. His use of private investigators. And about Gennifer Flowers and other instances of what his top aide, Betsey Wright, calls the "bimbo eruptions."

The American people have a right to know. But the media has not used their freedom to tell the truth about Bill Clinton.

I have.

Second, Ron Brown, the Chairman of the Democratic National Committee, resorted to censorship in order to ban me from the nation's air waves during the fall presidential campaign. Mr. Brown wrote to 1,500 broadcast stations to stop television ads I had prepared that told the truth about the Bill Clinton record. The Democratic Party

Chairman even threatened to take "legal action" to stop my efforts to expose this vital information. (See Appendix A.)

This was just one obstacle I faced; I will share with you a short list of other hurdles I jumped while preparing this book: my offices were burglarized during research for this project. Only my Clinton files were stolen. I had forged press releases distributed to the news media under my name. Ron Brown mailed his letter to nearly every broadcast outlet in the country suggesting that I be censored. I was sued unsuccessfully by Gennifer Flowers. I have had private telephone conversations illegally tape recorded and played on the CBS Evening News. I have had my office computer security breached by Modem. Despite these problems, I wanted Americans to know more about Bill Clinton than they otherwise might learn, and so I offer "Slick Willie."

Bill Clinton returned to Arkansas having spent his Oxford years looking at America through what Georgetown Professor Fr. Richard McSorley, who traveled with Bill Clinton in Europe, calls "peace eyes": the eyes of the international anti-American peace movement. In looking for the cause of world problems, Bill Clinton learned to blame America first.

He brought with him to Arkansas Hillary Rodham, the intelligent, aggressive, leftist activist who became First Lady of Arkansas when Bill Clinton won his first race for governor in 1978.

Hillary and Bill Clinton looked at Arkansas as a laboratory in which to enact the views they had learned as student activists in the 1960s. To them, Arkansas was a backwater, barely emerged into the twentieth century. Its taxes were too low. Its people were too traditional, too attached to family values. Hillary Rodham begrudgingly adopted her husband's family name to please the voters of Arkansas. She grimly set out to "modernize" Arkansas's approach to education while her husband rendered the state "up-to-date" by initiating a decade-long series of tax hikes.

Throughout the 1980s, Mr. Clinton courted the special interests while he raised taxes on the working man. He promoted his family and friends while embracing populist rhetoric. And he proclaimed as his "dream come true" an educational program that aimed to undermine the traditional moral values of Arkansas's "Gifted and Talented" children, and instead stuff them full of "up-to-date" modern values.

Now Bill Clinton wants to "do for America" what he "did for Arkansas." This book examines in detail his record and his promises.

I urge you to become familiar with the *whole* Bill Clinton story. I think you may find it deeply disturbing.

...cord the Federal... bank... plan... to... prevent Vietnam... but prognosis... to... understand... As for... as a remedy to it...tion while... for...im and render by... the great "Depression"... by financing... fiscal-aggressive tax hikes.

Though certainly... Mr. Clinton voiced the most evident wish to raise taxes on the wealthy... man. He proposed his small and... businesses... and raising popular theories. And he proclaimed... it... one is none that his government program that aimed to modernize the national health and insurance... and understood children, and increased... the fall of... high-tech-data... common values.

Now Bill Clinton wants to... for his future to take up the... Agenda... The book explains in detail his... soul and his promise.

I want you to become familiar with the future full Clinton story. I think you may find it useful then hope.

# Brave Men Died in Vietnam: Where Was Bill Clinton?

*"One of my roommates is a draft resister who is possibly under indictment and may never be able to go home again. He is one of the bravest, best men I know. . . . I decided to accept the draft in spite of my beliefs for one reason: to maintain my political viability within the system."*[1]

—Bill Clinton

*"Present polls show that there is the imminent danger to our country of a draft dodger becoming the Commander-in-Chief of the Armed Forces of the United States. While it is true, as Mr. Clinton has stated, that there were many others who avoided serving their country in the Vietnam war, they are not aspiring to be the President of the United States."*[2]

—Colonel Eugene Holmes

When Bill Clinton graduated from Georgetown University in 1968, all graduate school deferments had been abolished. His college deferment having expired, Mr. Clinton was declared 1-A ("Ready for duty"). But he didn't want to go to Vietnam. He wanted to pursue a Rhodes Scholarship at Oxford University. How could he get out of the draft?

Following is a chronology not just of political string-pulling, but of Bill Clinton's deliberate failure to notify his local draft board of a significant change in his military status—a lapse for which he could well have been convicted of a felony.

In addition, Mr. Clinton's involvement with a number of so-called "peace" organizations in England, at the time he was dodging the draft, further calls into question his position as U.S. Commander-in-Chief.

Bill Clinton's uncle, Raymond Clinton, was the first to pull strings to help his nephew evade the draft. Raymond Clinton was a prominent Hot Springs, Arkansas car dealer. According to Henry M. Britt, Raymond Clinton's attorney, Raymond Clinton persuaded Navy Lt. Commander Trice Ellis, Jr. to create a spot for Bill Clinton in the Naval Reserves even though all positions allotted to the Naval Reserves for Hot Springs, Arkansas were full at the time.

But two weeks after Commander Ellis found a spot for Bill Clinton, he wondered why the young Clinton had not shown up for the pre-induction physical. The Commander called Raymond Clinton and asked, "What happened to that boy?" Commander Ellis still recalls Raymond Clinton's response: "Don't worry about it . . . He won't be coming down. It's been all taken care of."[3]

Other strings were being pulled for Bill Clinton. Raymond Corrado, a member of the Hot Springs draft board, told the *Los Angeles Times* that an aide to Senator J. William Fulbright (D-Arkansas)—the Senator for whom Bill Clinton had previously worked—called to ask Mr. Corrado to "give every consideration" to keep Mr. Clinton out of the draft. Mr. Corrado was annoyed "something terrible" by what he regarded as a request for special treatment.[4]

The Hot Springs, Arkansas draft board ultimately decided, in effect, to postpone Bill Clinton's induction for nearly a year in order to allow him to continue his studies at Oxford. "As old as he was, he would have been at the top of the list" to be drafted, Opal Ellis, the Hot Springs draft board's executive secretary, told The *Wall Street Journal.* "We were proud to have a Hot Springs boy with a Rhodes scholarship," she added, so "the board was very lenient with him . . . we gave him more than he was entitled to."[5]

There is no solid evidence that Bill Clinton knew about his uncle's efforts to keep him out of war. Senator Fulbright has not disclosed his office's role in the affair. Raymond Clinton is now dead. But Henry Britt, Raymond Clinton's attorney, recently told the *Los Angeles Times* that "of course Billy knew" about his uncle's lobbying.[6] At any rate, there cannot be any dispute about the fact that Bill Clinton received treatment that was highly unusual. The *Los Angeles Times* reported that Bill Clinton "was the only man of his prime draft age classified 1-A by that board in 1968 whose pre-induction physical examination was put off for 10½ months—more than twice as long as anyone else and more than five times longer than most area men of comparable eligibility."[7]

But even Bill Clinton could not delay the draft indefinitely. He received a draft notice in April 1969[8], and his efforts to dodge the draft became frantic. He had to find some alternative.

Opal Ellis recalls that after Bill Clinton's return from Oxford in the summer of 1969, he came to Hot Springs and confronted her. According to Ms. Ellis, Clinton came to her office and "told me he was too well educated to go" to Vietnam. Ms. Ellis said that Mr. Clinton told her "he was going to fix my wagon [and] pull every string he could think of" to avoid military service.[9]

Bill Clinton then sought to avoid being drafted as an enlisted man. He tried to enter the Air Force and Navy officer programs, but failed physicals for both programs because he had bad eyesight and poor hearing.

So Mr. Clinton made an agreement in the summer of 1969 to enter the ROTC program at the University of Arkansas Law School. Colonel Eugene Holmes, Commander of the Army ROTC unit at the University of Arkansas, apparently sent a 1-D deferment ("Member of reserve component or student taking military training") to Mr. Clinton's local draft board, after which Mr. Clinton returned to Oxford. "I thought he was going to finish a month or two in England and then come back to the University of Arkansas," Colonel Holmes told the *Wall Street Journal* on February 6, 1992. Giving Mr. Clinton a 1-D deferment for a *full year* was not something Colonel Holmes says he would have done; "that wouldn't have been ethical."[10]

But while Mr. Clinton told the military and his draft board one version of his plans, he shared with his mother, Virginia, another plan—to finish at Oxford and go to Yale Law School. "I was under the impression when he came home from Oxford he was going to go to Yale," she recalls.[11]

What happened next can best be summarized in Bill Clinton's own words, written to Colonel Holmes in a December 3, 1969 letter that Bill Clinton sent *two days after* receiving a high number (311) in the new draft lottery.

(Note: It was Bill Clinton's ROTC letter of intent that spared him from getting drafted during the critical months of summer and early fall of 1969. Once he received his number (311), he no longer needed the deferment. It was only then, *two days after* Mr. Clinton knew that his high lottery number virtually guaranteed he would not be drafted, that he wrote to Colonel Holmes announcing that he would not enter the University of Arkansas ROTC program.)

"I am sorry to be so long in writing," Mr. Clinton explained. "I know I promised to let you hear from me at least once a month, and from now on you will, but I have had to have some time to think about this first letter. Almost daily since my return to England I have thought about writing, about what I want to and ought to say."

"First, I want to thank you, not just for saving me from the draft, but for being so kind to me last summer . . ."

"After I signed the ROTC letter of intent I began to wonder whether the compromise I had made with myself was not more objectionable than the draft would have been, because I had no interest in the ROTC program in itself, and all I seemed to have done was to protect myself from physical harm. Also, I began to think I had deceived you, not by lies—there were none—but by failing to tell you all the things I'm writing now . . ."

"At that time, after we had made our agreement and you had sent my 1-D deferment to my draft board, the anguish and loss of self-regard and self-respect really set in. I hardly slept for weeks and kept going by eating compulsively and reading until exhaustion brought sleep. Finally, on September 12, I stayed up all night writing a letter to the chairman of my draft board, saying basically what is in the preceding paragraph, thanking him for trying to help in a case where he really couldn't and stating that I couldn't do the ROTC after all and would he please draft me as soon as possible. I never mailed the letter but I did carry it on me every day until I got on the plane to return to England."[12] (See Appendix B.)

These excerpts raise a number of questions: Why did Bill Clinton promise to let Colonel Holmes "hear from [him] at least once a month?" Was this supposed to be some sort of "provisional" or "informal" ROTC enrollment? If so, this was explicitly forbidden by the ROTC regulations [32 CFR 562.25(f) (1969)].

Did Bill Clinton write any subsequent "monthly" letters to Colonel Holmes after he promised to do so in his December 3, 1969 letter?

Did Bill Clinton ever intend to join the ROTC unit? If so, when and under what conditions?

Colonel Holmes addresses some of these concerns in an affidavit he released to the American public in September 1992: "I believe that [Bill Clinton] purposely deceived me, using the possibility of joing the ROTC as a ploy to work with the draft board to delay his induction and get a new draft classification." (See Appendix C for Colonel Holmes's full affidavit.)

The most important question may be when, if ever, did Bill Clinton give *written* notice to his local draft board that he was not a member of the Army ROTC unit at the University of Arkansas, a status for which he purportedly received his 1-D deferment.

Under the Selective Service laws in force at the time, Bill Clinton had a continuing legal duty to keep his local board informed of his occupational and military status, and to report any change in such status to his local draft board "within ten days after it occurs" [32 C.F.R. 1641.7 (a) (1969)]. Both Mr. Clinton and the ROTC Commanding Officer (or whoever else actually filed the request for Clinton's 1-D deferment) had a duty within ten days after it actually occurred to report to the local draft board *in writing* "any fact that might result in the registrant being placed in a different classification, such as, but not limited to, any change in his occupational, marital, military, or dependency status, or in his physical condition."[32 C.F.R. 1625.1(b) (1969)]

Other draft registrants of Bill Clinton's age were prosecuted and convicted for failure to notify their draft boards of changes in status. For example, in the 1972 case of *United States v. Bruckman*, a draft registrant had attempted to obtain a 1-D deferment (like Bill Clinton's) by joining what he thought was an Illinois National Guard Unit. In fact, the Guard Unit did not exist and the 1-D deferment likewise was bogus. These facts came to light in a subsequent FBI investigation. The United States Court of Appeals for the Seventh Circuit upheld Mr. Bruckman's conviction for failing "to give notice to his Local Board of a change in his military status (i.e., that he was not a member of the Illinois National Guard)."[13]

If Bill Clinton did provide written notice to his local draft board, the local draft board and Bill Clinton should have a record of it. If the written notice occurred on or after September 23, 1969, or did not occur at all, Bill Clinton has himself, in effect, confessed to violating a felony criminal law. Since he never did join the ROTC unit, it is also likely that he violated a continuing legal duty to inform his local draft board of his status starting as early as August 7, 1969, when he was granted a 1-D deferment—ostensibly for a status he never achieved, i.e., membership in the ROTC.

The December letter is revealing not only because it implicates criminal culpability in 1969, but because it reveals a flaw in Bill Clinton's character that crops up repeatedly throughout his life. Bill Clinton, over the years, has repeatedly evaded tough questions, or offered partial truths, instead of being forthright and honest. The issue of Bill Clinton and the draft, for example, is an old charge;

it was first raised in his 1978 race for governor, when Billy Geren, a retired Lieutenant Colonel, charged that Bill Clinton was a "draft dodger"[14] for canceling the ROTC agreement.

Even though much was known about Bill Clinton's non-existent war record as far back as 1978, one vital piece of evidence was missing—the letter he wrote to Colonel Holmes. Mr. Clinton was thus able to disguise his efforts to avoid the draft for more than a decade.

The *Arkansas Gazette* reported on October 20, 1978 that Bill Clinton claimed "the agreement was never sent to Washington and he was not deferred."[15] That claim is only partly true; Bill Clinton was, in the end, not deferred from the draft because the Hot Springs draft board re-classified him 1-A on October 31, 1969.

Bill Clinton's efforts to shade the truth about his avoidance of the draft raise serious questions about his credibility. "It took him months to reveal all of what is now known about his draft record—and sometimes only after repeated questioning from news organizations,"[16] reported the *Washington Post*'s Dan Balz.

1. Bill Clinton's letter to Colonel Holmes, December 3, 1969.
2. Colonel Eugene Holmes' September 1992 Affidavit (See Appendix C).
3. *Los Angeles Times,* September 2, 1992.
4. *ibid.*
5. *Wall Street Journal,* February 6, 1992.
6. *Los Angeles Times,* September 2, 1992.
7. *ibid.*
8. *Human Events*, August 22, 1992.
9. *Wall Street Journal,* February 6, 1992.
10. *ibid.*
11. *ibid.*

12. Bill Clinton's letter to Colonel Holmes, December 3, 1969 (See Appendix B).
13. 466 F.2d 754 (7th Cir. 1992).
14. *Boston Globe*, September 6, 1992.
15. *Arkansas Gazette*, September 6, 1992.
16. *Washington Post*, September 8, 1992.

# Peacenik for President:
# Bill Clinton's Protest Years

*"As I was waiting for the ceremony to begin, Bill Clinton of Georgetown, then studying as a Rhodes Scholar at Oxford, came up and welcomed me. He was one of the [protest] organizers."*[1]

—FATHER MCSORLEY

*"I went to Washington to work in the national headquarters of the moratorium, then to England to organize the Americans here for demonstrations October 15th and November 16th."*[2]

—BILL CLINTON

Bill Clinton's draft record dogged him since serious questions were first raised in the *Wall Street Journal* in February 1992. Aside from draft-dodging, there is a fundamental question about Mr. Clinton's antiwar activities from his Rhodes Scholar days that he never fully addressed: his direct connections with "peace" groups that were operating openly as an arm of the international department of the Soviet Union's KGB.

To learn this story we turn to Father Richard McSorley, a Jesuit priest and Professor of Peace Studies who has taught at Georgetown University since Bill Clinton's student days. Father McSorley's memoir about his international travels with the pacifist movement, *Peace Eyes,* was published in 1977.

*Peace Eyes* begins: "When I got off the train in Oslo, Norway, I met Bill Clinton of Georgetown University. He asked if he could go with me visiting peace people. We visited the Oslo Peace Institute, talked with conscientious objectors, with peace groups, and with university students. At the end of the day as Bill was preparing to leave, he commented, 'This is a great way to see a country.' "[3]

Father McSorley was impressed with Bill Clinton's words: "to see a country with a peace focus, through the eyes of peace people, is a good way to travel, a good way to see the country and the world," he wrote.[4]

As a Rhodes Scholar, Bill Clinton learned to see the world—including his native America—through the eyes of the international peace movement. The details of that perspective and its influence on his world view are not widely known. They should give serious pause to his supporters, regardless of their feelings about his response to service in the U.S. armed forces.

Father McSorley traveled from Norway to England. "On November 15, 1969, I participated in the British moratorium against the Vietnam War in front of the U.S. Embassy at Grosvenor Square in London. Even the appearance of the Embassy stressed the over exaggerated nature of America's power. . . . The total effect of architecture and decor says to the passer-by, 'America is the biggest and greatest power on the globe.' "[5]

"That day in November about 500 Britons and Americans were meeting to express their sorrow at America's misuse of power in Vietnam. . . . Most of them carried signs which said, Americans out of Vietnam."[6]

Father McSorley goes on to describe vividly the demonstration and its profound effect on him.

"The activities in London supporting the second stage of the moratorium and the March of Death in Washington were initiated by Group 68 (Americans in Britain). This group had the support of British peace organizations, including the Committee on Nuclear Disarmament, the British Peace Council, and the International Committee for Disarmament and Peace."[7]

Then comes this revelation from Father McSorley: "The next day I joined with about 500 other people for the interdenominational service. Most of them were young, and many of them were Americans. As I was waiting for the ceremony to begin, Bill Clinton of Georgetown, then studying as a Rhodes Scholar at Oxford, came up and welcomed me. He was one of the organizers."[8]

This prosaic, thorough depiction of those events puts Bill Clinton squarely in the lead of demonstrations supported by the British Peace Council or Committee, an affiliate of the World Peace Council and as obvious a front group for the Soviet Union's KGB as any that ever was.

At the time of these demonstrations, brave young men without the connections of Bill Clinton were dying in Vietnam. They died at the hand of an enemy who daily expressed gratitude for the activities of the fifth column in which Bill Clinton proudly served. In anticipation of the demonstration organized by Mr. Clinton, the Minister of Culture for the Communist Government of North Vietnam, Hoang Minh Giam, said, " 'The Vietnamese warmly acclaim and support with all their strength the struggle engaged' by opponents of the war."[9]

Now, Bill Clinton at Oxford was no naïf. He was a calculating political activist, already confirmed in his ambition and taking great care to preserve what he considered his "political viability."[10] His leadership in a movement operating under the direct aegis and support

FLOYD G. BROWN • 13

of one of the most notorious Communist front organizations in Europe can hardly be discounted as innocent or ignorant meanderings.

Clearly, Bill Clinton took his position on the war with great prudential care and reflection. It was at Oxford that Mr. Clinton gathered around him the advisors who still constitute the senior leadership of his campaign. His actions were deliberate and calculated.

In his September 1992 affidavit, Colonel Eugene Holmes offers this reflection: "When I consider the calabre, the bravery, and the patriotism of the fine young soldiers whose deaths I have witnessed, and others whose funerals I have attended. . . . When I reflect on not only the willingness but eagerness that so many of them displayed in their earnest desire to defend and serve their country, it is untenable and incomprehensible to me that a man who was not merely unwilling to serve his country, but actually protested against its military, should ever be in the position of Commander-in-Chief of our armed Forces."[11]

1. *Peace Eyes,* page 23.
2. Bill Clinton's letter to Colonel Holmes (See Appendix B).
3. Peace Eyes, page.
4. *ibid.*
5. *ibid.*
6. *ibid.*
7. *ibid.*
8. *ibid.*
9. *The Times London,* October 14, 1969.
10. Bill Clinton's letter to Colonel Holmes (See Appendix B).
11. Colonel Eugene Holmes September 1992 Affidavit (See Appendix C).

# Marijuana:
# To Inhale Or Not To Inhale

**Question:** "If you had it to do over again, would you inhale (marijuana)?"
**Clinton:** "Sure, if I could. I tried before."
—Mtv's "Choose or Lose Special" June 16, 1992

After dodging questions about his drug use for *years*, Bill Clinton finally admitted in April 1992, during the New York primary, that he tried marijuana while a graduate student at Oxford, but added the qualifier that, while he had smoked marijuana, he "didn't inhale."

Try to follow this:

In 1986, Bill Clinton was asked "Have you ever used drugs?" He said he had not.

In 1989, Mr. Clinton said he had never used illegal drugs while an adult in Arkansas.

In his 1990 gubernatorial contest, Mr. Clinton said he "never violated the drug laws of the state" of Arkansas.

In 1991, *Arkansas Gazette* reporter Scott Morris narrowed the question, asking Mr. Clinton if he ever tried marijuana in college. The Governor again denied he had used illicit drugs: "The answer to that question is no. That's the question you asked and I'll give you the answer."[1]

In a 1991 speech at the National Press Club, Bill Clinton said he hadn't violated state or federal drug laws.

When Bill Clinton finally admitted that he had used marijuana, it was only because journalists asked him if he had smoked marijuana while in graduate school and/or if he had violated international drug laws. "I've never broken a state law," Mr. Clinton said in March 1992, "but when I was in England I experimented with marijuana a time or two, and I didn't like it. I didn't inhale it, and never tried it again."[2]

When asked why he had not disclosed this information before, Mr. Clinton said, "Nobody's ever asked me that question point blank."[3]

"The Clinton pattern has been to shade the truth, to be a little too cute, to answer questions with lawyer-like tergiversations," observes columnist Robert Novak. "His seeming denial of youthful marijuana use until he was asked the precisely correct question, and then his absurd claim that he did not 'inhale,' have become symbolic of what's wrong with him."[4]

The issue is not really whether Bill Clinton puffed marijuana. The issue is *why* he spent so much time and energy covering up the truth. Bill Clinton spent years coming up with increasingly strained and hair-splitting answers as to whether he smoked marijuana. That is how Mr. Clinton responds to direct questions about his character. Can America trust him?

It seems that he further disqualified himself as a good role model for America's young people with his flip remark on "Music Television" ("MTV") that if he "had it to do over again," he would inhale. Is this a proper message for a presidential candidate to send young people?

As *Arkansas Democrat Gazette* columnist John R. Starr

lamented during the Democratic primaries: "By anybody's reckoning, we are now faced with nominating a confessed philanderer and pot smoker and a proven liar."[5]

1. *Spectrum,* April 8, 1992.
2. *New York Times,* March 30, 1992.
3. *ibid.*
4. *The American Spectator,* June 1992.
5. *Arkansas Democrat Gazette,* March 31, 1992.

# Tom Cat in The Mansion: Twelve Years as Arkansas Governor

*"Bill Clinton is like an old Tom Cat. It doesn't matter how many times you throw him off the roof. He always lands on his feet."*

—ANONYMOUS POLITICAL PUNDIT

Bill Clinton's record as Arkansas governor is a record of raising taxes, pardoning violent criminals, repeatedly involving himself in conflicts of interest, giving drug dealers fat state contracts, and allowing campaign contributors to foul the land.

When Bill Clinton first took gubernatorial office in 1979, he promised the voters that he would bring change. He told the voters he was no liberal. But Frank Lady, an opponent in the Democratic primary, charged that Bill Clinton was "the most liberal politician to ever come out of Arkansas."[1]

Around the shielded governor circled charges of conflicts of interest. In 1979, a state auditor discovered that during his tenure as state attorney general, Mr. Clinton oversaw what the *Arkansas Gazette* described as "apparently haphazard accounting procedures and inadequately explained expense reimbursements."[2] The Attorney General's office had 12 checking accounts, and funds from one account had been used to pay debts in other accounts. For example, Mr. Clinton's staffers routinely used checks from federal fund accounts to pay off debts in state accounts.

On top of that, the audit charged that workers from the Clinton campaign used state gasoline credit cards to fuel their vehicles while campaigning for Mr. Clinton's gubernatorial race.

Mr. Clinton used patronage far more ruthlessly than his predecessors. "Governor Clinton Takes Patronage to New Depths," reported the *Arkansas Gazette* in 1979. Patronage, Mr. Clinton told the *Gazette*'s Brenda Tirey, was a way of making bureaucracy more responsive. The governor's staff members were more blunt: "We want to keep our supporters and friends involved," said Rudy Moore, a top Clinton aide. "We want to make them feel they're part of state government." Mr. Moore was subsequently appointed by Governor Clinton to a judgeship in Fayetteville, Arkansas.

But what concerned voters even more than Governor Clinton's staff and patronage were his stands on issues such as taxes and crime.

During his first term as governor, Bill Clinton commuted 44 life sentences of prisoners. One of them, murderer James Surridge, murdered again shortly after he was released, and the incident became a major controversy. Another lifer whose sentence was commuted, Guy Laverne Kuehn, only remained in prison because the widow and relatives of the man he had murdered gathered petitions urging that he remain in jail.

Coming into his first reelection bid in 1980, Governor Clinton thought he had an invincible lead, and polls showed that one week before election day, he was twenty points ahead. But Republican opponent Frank White successfully hammered him on the tax and crime issues. In the end, voters ousted Mr. Clinton for his liberal positions and his overall arrogance.

In an analysis following the Clinton defeat, *Arkansas Gazette* writers John Brummett and Steele Hays concluded that Bill Clinton was too evasive with the voters. While Frank White, for example, answered a questionnaire from the Moral Majority, Bill Clinton "decided not to answer the questionnaire and said it was impossible to give 'yes' or 'no' answers."

Messrs. Brummett and Hays wrote that, despite his efforts to camouflage his beliefs, Bill Clinton was too liberal for the voters of Arkansas. Not only did his "liberal, Eastern establishment reputation" hurt him, they reflected, but "voters saw Mr. Clinton as arrogant, aloof, inaccessible, or egotistical. The national attention he has received instead of helping may have hurt him, causing voters to view him as overly ambitious and being more interested in his political future than in them."[3]

While out of power, Mr. Clinton thought about what caused his defeat. He told journalists who would listen that he did not believe all federal funds were automatically good. "Several times as governor," he told the *Pine Bluff Commercial* in 1981, "I took federal money for programs not worth a hill of beans because I couldn't see it go to New Jersey."[4]

But Mr. Clinton knew that his political career was not over. "There was absolutely no doubt that I would run again," he told *The Washington Post*. "The very moment I was conceding defeat my mind was spinning with ideas about what I had to do to stay active and get back."[5]

So the Arkansas voters in 1981 were regaled with advertisements in which Bill Clinton told them he was sorry for his performance in his first term, and that he promised not to be arrogant and mean. Along with his law partner, Bruce Lindsey—who served as co-chairman of the Clinton for President Campaign, Mr. Clinton roamed shopping centers, approaching voters with what Hillary Clinton called "confessionals in the supermarket aisles."[6] Commercials reminded voters that Bill Clinton was a weak and sorry man, and they broadcast his new message: "I learned that you can't lead without listening."

The consummate politician, Mr. Clinton even campaigned in his Immanuel Baptist Church, a white mainline church in an increasingly black section of Little Rock. Every Sunday, viewers of the church's popular broadcasts would see the minister—and Bill Clinton lustily singing in the choir right behind him. "When the church's broadcasts became a minor issue in a later election," Clinton biographers Charles F. Allen and Jonathan Portis report, "church officials and Clinton denied that it had been a calculated maneuver."[7]

In February 1982, Mr. Clinton announced what voters had known for months. He wanted his old job back. He had repackaged himself. His hair was neater and shorter. Hillary Rodham declared that she was now "Hillary Clinton."

When election time came, Bill Clinton triumphed by a 55-45 percent margin. He was the first Arkansas governor to regain his office after losing it.

In 1984 and 1986, Mr. Clinton scored easy victories against weak opposition. In 1984, he beat Woody Freeman, a construction executive, by a 64-36 margin. In 1986, Mr. Clinton beat Frank White in a rematch.

Governor Clinton did not have to run in 1988 because Arkansas had shifted from a two-year to a four-year term—a change he had assiduously promoted. (It was certainly convenient for Bill Clinton to be freed from gubernatorial races during presidential election years.)

In 1990, Mr. Clinton met his toughest challenge in nearly a decade. Business executive Sheffield Nelson put up a fierce fight complete with buttons proclaiming "Ten Years is Enough!"

Governor Clinton faced real trouble this time. Wherever he went, voters asked him one question: Governor, if you are re-elected, will you raise my taxes?

Sheffield Nelson took a pledge that he would not raise taxes if elected governor, and he predicted that Bill Clinton, if elected, would both raise taxes and run for president. Governor Clinton could not take the tax pledge because he had raised taxes consistently in his first eight years as governor and would raise them again in the following two years.

To defeat Sheffield Nelson's strong challenge, Governor Clinton resorted to old-fashioned tactics. He borrowed money for the first time in years. And on Election Day, the *Arkansas Democrat* reported, voters in the poorer areas of Little Rock received an old-fashioned treat—free fried chicken and a ride if they made it to the polls, courtesy of the Clinton campaign's "get the vote out" efforts.[8]

Governor Clinton prevailed over Mr. Nelson with a 57-43 margin. This was Mr. Clinton's smallest winning percentage since returning to the governorship.

Then, despite this narrow victory, Bill Clinton raised taxes 53 times in the next legislative session for a total of $323 million.

He also broke a vow he had issued during the campaign against Mr. Nelson.

In a statewide debate, Governor Clinton had been asked the following question: "Will you guarantee all of us that if re-elected there is absolutely, positively, no way that you will run for any other political office, and that you will serve your term out in full?"

"You bet!" Governor Clinton replied. "I told you when I announced for Governor, I intend to run and that's what I'm going to do. I'm going to serve four years. I made that decision when I decided to run. If you listen to all these political comments they will tell you that no one much outside of Arkansas believes I could do anything else. When I decided to run for Governor, I decided to serve four years as Governor."

"I'm being considered for the candidate for Governor," Mr. Clinton insisted. "That's the job I want, that's the job I'll do for the next four years."[9]

Technically, Bill Clinton does not say that he will not run for President, but that "I decided to serve four years as Governor." Mr. Clinton of course knew that he did not have to give up the governorship to run for president.

However, as with Mr. Clinton's statements on the draft and his drug use, double-talk covered up the truth. (Finally, in April 1992, Governor Clinton declared himself "released" from this pledge.)[10]

When Americans went to the voting booths in November 1992, most were unaware of Governor Clinton's record of broken promises as Arkansas's chief executive, and his declining popularity in his home state.

1. *Arkansas Gazette*, April 30, 1978.
2. *Arkansas Gazette*, March 2, 1979.
3. *Arkansas Gazette*, November 6, 1980.
4. "Pine Bluff Commercial", July 24, 1981.
5. *Washington Post*, July 14, 1992.
6. *ibid.* July 14, 1992.
7. *Comeback Kid*, page 75.
8. *Arkansas Democratic Gazette*, November 18, 1990.
9. *Comeback Kid*, page 135.
10. *Texarkana Gazette*, April 6, 1992.

# "Billion-Dollar Bill": Arkansas's Tax Kingpin

*"I care more about this [1987 tax increase] than anything else. I think it's more important to the future of our state than anything else and I'm prepared to go on, and on, and on, and on, until we get some resolution of it."*[1]

—Governor BILL CLINTON

*"It's hard to think of anything except motherhood and apple pie that the Legislature didn't tax."*[2]

—COLUMNIST JOHN R. STARR
THE ARKANSAS DEMOCRAT

*"[Arkansas's tax increases] show a level of discipline, commitment, and looking to the future that makes us feel better."*[3]

—GOVERNOR BILL CLINTON

Bill Clinton was governor of Arkansas for twelve years, from 1978 until 1980, and from 1982 on. He is certainly a man who loves big government. In fact, he loves it so much that during his tenure as governor, he doubled the state's budget and more than doubled state taxes. In 1980, when Bill Clinton raised the Arkansas budget over a billion dollars for the first time, critics derisively called him "Billion Dollar Bill."

Bill Clinton has repeatedly asked Americans to consider his record when deciding whether or not to support his programs. Here is that tax-and-spend record, taken from *Congressional Quarterly*:[4]

| Fiscal Year | State Taxes (in millions) | % increase | State Spending (in millions) | % increase |
| --- | --- | --- | --- | --- |
| 1979 | 995 | 7.0 | 1,897 | 12.6 |
| 1980 | 1,161 | 16.6 | 2,148 | 13.2 |
| 1983 | 1,338 | 9.3 | 2,488 | 5.3 |
| 1984 | 1,541 | 8.3 | 2,636 | 5.9 |
| 1985 | 1,745 | 12.6 | 3,018 | 14.5 |
| 1986 | 1,827 | 8.4 | 3,355 | 11.2 |
| 1987 | 1,889 | 7.3 | 3,473 | 3.5 |
| 1988 | 2,022 | 1.8 | 3,570 | 2.8 |
| 1989 | 2,172 | 8.6 | 3,840 | 7.6 |
| 1990 | 2,261 | 4.9 | 4,223 | 10.0 |

Every year that Bill Clinton was Arkansas's governor, he increased government spending and taxes with the regularity of a clock. The Arkansas tax burden is now 127 percent greater than when Mr. Clinton was first elected governor, and the amount of government spending is 122 percent greater. The Arkansas budget could easily be cut. In fiscal year 1982, for example, Republican Governor Frank White cut taxes and increased state government spending by only 0.3 percent.

But during his 12 years as governor, Bill Clinton all but destroyed Arkansas's low-tax tradition. In his authoritative analysis of Governor Clinton's spending patterns, Stephen Moore of the Cato Institute reveals these facts:

- Governor Clinton raised the sales tax from 3 percent to 4.5 percent.
- He raised the corporate income tax from a maximum rate of 6 percent to a maximum rate of 6.5 percent.
- He raised the gasoline tax from 9.5 cents per gallon to 18.5 cents per gallon.
- By 1990, the average Arkansas family of four had to pay over $1,500 more in taxes each year than they did before Bill Clinton became governor.
- By continuing the sales tax on food and nearly doubling the gasoline tax, Governor Clinton's tax policies hurt poor people the hardest by taxing the food they need to eat and the gasoline they need to get to work.

Under Bill Clinton's direction, sales taxes were added to used cars, mobile homes, and recreational vehicles for the first time in Arkansas history. "Clinton's fiscal record is below average in most categories," Mr. Moore concludes, "and in some areas it is near the bottom."

During "the Clinton era the state tax system has become more regressive," the *Arkansas Gazette* admits. "It has become, step by step, a pretty bad system, stacked against the ordinary taxpayer and consumer."

Bill Clinton's propensity to raise taxes was a major reason why he suffered defeat in his 1980 re-election bid. In his first term as governor, Mr. Clinton persuaded the state legislature to pass a bill doubling the fees on car tags from $15 to $30. This tax outraged voters for two reasons. First, getting a car tag registered in Arkansas is a painful ordeal. After standing in a long line, the driver must prove that he owns the car; prove that he has paid property taxes; prove that he has insurance on the car; prove that his car has passed a state inspection within thirty days; and submit an assessment of the property taxes he anticipates paying in the next year. All of this is preface to payment of the tag fee.

"People in the countryside were outraged when they'd finally get to the end of the line and be hit with the increase," wrote *Arkansas Gazette* reporter Ernest Dumas.[5] "That's all anybody would talk about for a year . . . To make matters worse, the title-transfer fee hit the rural poor hardest, because they often bought an old car, drove it until it broke down and then bought another one." The fee increase, reported *Congressional Quarterly's* Rhodes Cook, "touched off a voter revolt in much of rural Arkansas from which [Clinton] has not fully recovered."[6]

By 1980, other Clinton reforms went awry. One program, known as SAWER (Special Alternative Wood Energy Resources) spent $62,000 to teach poor people how to cut wood and distribute it to the needy. The program trained six people who cut three cords of wood—at a cost to the taxpayer of more than $20,000 a cord.[7]

Following these and other embarrassments, Arkansans' enthusiasm for their young governor diminished, and he was voted out of office.

But Bill Clinton's enthusiasm for taxes remained undaunted, and when he returned to the governorship in 1983, one of his first acts was to raise the Arkansas sales tax—which hadn't been raised in 26 years—from three to four percent. (This was after he increased taxes on cigarettes, horse racing, and dog racing.)

Sales taxes in Arkansas are remarkably easy to raise. While it takes two-thirds of the state legislature to approve all other taxes, the sales tax only needs 50 percent plus one of the legislature to pass. Because of this quirk in the Arkansas constitution, Bill Clinton repeatedly raised sales taxes, even though they hurt the poor. When Mr. Clinton became governor, 27 percent of Arkansas's state income came from sales taxes; by 1990, the figure had increased to 35.5 percent.

In 1983, Bill Clinton claimed that the budget had been cut to its limit. "We've cut, cut, and cut," he said "and we can cut some more. But if we're going to fund some of these programs, if we're going to make these sides of the ledger come out even, we've got to raise some money."[8] In fact, few cuts were made, and they were swiftly reversed once Mr. Clinton had won the tax increase.

The Arkansas Fairness Council, a coalition of black organizations, labor unions, and women's groups, pleaded with Mr. Clinton to exempt food from the sales tax increase. He refused, but promised the Council he would support a sales tax rebate for low-income taxpayers in exchange for passage of his sales tax increase. But after Mr. Clinton got his tax-increase bill passed in the Arkansas House of Representatives, he announced that he had changed his mind and that he was opposing all rebates.

Bill Clinton's tax flip-flop embittered many Arkansas activists. "We counted on him," said Brownie Ledbetter, president of the Arkansas Fairness Council. Ms. Ledbetter, who had been a long-time Clinton supporter, told the *Wall Street Journal*: "We stood there and watched while he broke his word. It happened whiz-bang."[9]

The Arkansas state legislature meets only every other year, so Governor Clinton could not raise taxes in 1984 and 1986. Indeed, in 1985, buoyed by the booming economic growth from Ronald Reagan's first term, he gave Arkansas corporations a major rebate on sales taxes, provided they stay in the state. But in 1987, Governor Clinton was back, trying to raise taxes again.

As in earlier tax campaigns, Bill Clinton contended that tax increases were necessary to save the schools. He claimed at first that he was "open to all options" except across-the-board sales tax increases. "I would want either some break for food or a combination of them and relief for low-income people," he told the *Arkansas Gazette* on March 26, 1987.[10]

Two days later, he changed his mind, calling for a quarter-of-a-cent sales tax increase. He maintained the increase was necessary to mandate tough state standards for schools. He even suggested that voters be grateful for the tax increase because it showed "a level of discipline, commitment, and looking to the future that will make us feel better about the future of our state."[11]

Bill Clinton was so enthusiastic about raising taxes that he launched a series of radio advertisements that pleaded: "We don't have enough money to fund the standards today because the economic problems on our farms and in our rural counties have depressed state revenues."[12] (Translation: "High tax rates meant that businesses have failed to pay taxes, so we need to increase taxes even more.")

Despite the colorful manner in which Mr. Clinton disguised his tax pleas, surprisingly few citizens called their legislators to request higher taxes. The governor said he felt besieged during his fight for a tax increase: "I sort of feel like General Grant at Vicksburg. They said he was drunk, no good, he didn't have any sense. But he won the battle because he came to fight and stayed and stayed and stayed . . . I care more about this [tax increase] than anything else. I think it's more important to the future of our state than anything else and I'm prepared to go on, and on, and on, and on, until we get some resolution of it."[13]

Even the prospect of Governor Clinton spending months in an empty legislature did not pressure the legislators to change their minds. They refused to increase the sales tax, although they did increase corporate taxes and taxes for renting property.

One year later, the big 1987 tax increases brought an unexpected result. The state was receiving more money from taxes than it expected, $35 million instead of $25 million. State Rep. Richard Barclay made a proposal that was, for the Clinton years, highly unusual: the state should return the extra money to the people. Bill Clinton opposed this. As the *Arkansas Democrat* reported, Mr. Clinton believed that "making any adjustments [returning or lowering taxes] would probably amount to giving money back to higher income taxpayers at a time when the state is seeking ways to give more tax breaks to the lower income taxpayers."[14]

In 1991, having survived his battle with gubernatorial opponent Sheffield Nelson, Bill Clinton did what Mr. Nelson had predicted: "raise and spend" taxpayer money. By the end of the session, Governor Clinton had convinced the state legislature to raise the sales tax, boost the gasoline tax by five cents, add one cent to the cigarette tax, and make sure that buyers of used cars had to pay taxes.

Governor Clinton was jubilant. The session, he said, "had been an unbelievable success."[15] Other politicians were more honest. "A lot of people will say, 'Is there anything you didn't tax this time?'"[16] said state Rep. Pat Flanagan.

"It is hard to think of anything except motherhood and apple pie that the Legislature didn't tax," observed *Arkansas Democrat* columnist John R. Starr. "From the point of view of a tax-and-spender, it was, indeed, the best session in history."[17]

Mr. Starr also observed that while appalled voters had previously called their governor "Billion Dollar Bill," with his $1.9 billion annual budget, "it won't be long before we can start calling Clinton 'Two Billion Dollar Bill.' "

1. *Arkansas Gazette,* March 31, 1987.
2. *Arkansas Democrat,* June 29, 1991.
3. *Arkansas Gazette,* March 28, 1987.
4. *Congressional Quarterly,* January 11, 1992.
5. *Comeback Kid,* page 62.
6. *Congressional Quarterly,* January 11, 1992.
7. *Comeback Kid,* page 65.
8. *Arkansas Gazette,* February 18, 1983.
9. *Wall Street Journal,* March 19, 1992.
10. *Arkansas Gazette,* March 26, 1987.
11. *Arkansas Gazette,* March 28, 1987.
12. *ibid.*
13. *ibid.*
14. *Arkansas Democrat Gazette,* June 26, 1988.
15. *Arkansas Democrat Gazette,* June 29, 1991.
16. *ibid.*
17. *ibid.*

# The Arkansas Education Swindle

*"Many of Arkansas's brightest young minds were being held back by religious, conservative, overbearing training at home, and this is our first shot at them."*[1]
—BRUCE HAGGARD
DIRECTOR OF ARKANSAS'S GOVERNOR'S SCHOOL

*"I would like to have incorporated into our curriculum a unit on alternative [homosexual] lifestyles . . . this hasn't been made public yet . . . you know we are often subject to all sorts of lawsuits and complaints if we get into anything that deals with values or morals or ethics."*[2]
—MARGIE POWELL, YOUTH-AT-RISK DIRECTOR
ARKANSAS DEPARTMENT OF EDUCATION

Bill Clinton places a lot of emphasis on education.

As governor of Arkansas, he focused on education because it gave him the freedom and the power to raise taxes, to destroy local neighborhood autonomy, and to make a name for himself in national politics.

The real question for Americans is, did Mr. Clinton's efforts to improve education paid off? For the most part, they did not.

In 1983, Mr. Clinton kicked off his second term as governor by appointing a blue-ribbon commission, chaired by Hillary Clinton, to study how Arkansas schools could be improved. The commission recommended the conventional wisdom of the day: longer school days; stricter standards for graduation; competency tests for students; and consolidation of school districts. The most controversial recommendation insisted that teachers be required to pass mandatory competency tests or face expulsion from the classroom. Although the state legislature failed to approve school district consolidation, it approved all of the Governor's other reforms.

These reforms forced many Arkansas communities to raise their own local taxes to retain independence from the state. Because these tax hikes were adopted locally, not by the state government, Governor Clinton cannot be blamed directly for the rise in taxes.

Still, these reforms demonstrate how Bill Clinton used education as an excuse to raise taxes and increase the role of government in the daily lives of the people of Arkansas.[3]

The teacher competency tests led the Arkansas Education Association (AEA), the state affiliate of the National Education Association, to declare itself "at war" with Governor Clinton. The AEA had endorsed his opponent in the 1982 race—a lapse for which Mr. Clinton declared he would "beat their brains out" in retaliation— and it was livid about the competency tests. In the end, this "war" proved to be quite fruitful for Bill Clinton; his seeming independence from the teachers' unions earned him slots on national television talk shows (such as Phil Donahue) for the first time.

Governor Clinton's refusal to knuckle under to the teachers' unions won him popularity. But when the teachers' test was issued in 1985, it proved to be so easy that two *Arkansas Gazette* reporters and a student intern who sneaked in to take the test scored well. In fact, *TIME* magazine reports that 93 percent of teachers passed the test the first time, and an additional four percent passed after taking the test a second time. Only three percent of the teachers who took the test flunked, and a majority of those teachers were put back to work in part-time or substitute positions.

As for Governor Clinton's other reforms, they did little to improve Arkansas education. Most education experts now agree that imposing top-down reform strategies is ineffective. Making graduation requirements "tougher" sounds great, but it does little to modify what teachers teach, or whether students learn.

Arkansas state spending on education rose from $1,330 per student in the 1980–81 school year to $2,760 per student in the 1990-91 school year. The average teacher salary rose from $13,527 in 1980–81, to $23,735 in 1990–91. Nearly 42 percent of the Arkansas state budget goes to education; only two other states spend proportionally more.

Yet test scores of Arkansan students remained dismal. While SAT scores improved slightly, only six percent of Arkansas high school students took the test. The preferred achievment test in Arkansas is the ACT test. Of the 28 states that use the ACT, Arkansas ranks 25th. In 1979, Arkansas's cumulative ACT ranking was 20th out of 28th nationwide. In 1990, 56 percent of Arkansas freshmen entering state colleges were forced to take remedial math courses.[4]

Mr. Clinton's feuds with the teachers' unions are long since over. In fact, the presidents of both the AEA and the National Education Association (NEA) now praise him highly.

Bill Clinton's "philosophy fits nicely into what I believe

the NEA is looking to for education in the year 2000," says NEA president Keith Geiger. "There's no doubt that he fits into what we are seeking in terms of education reform."[5]

A glimpse at this philosophy can be caught in Bill Clinton's Governor's School for the Talented and Gifted, a tax-funded summer school created in 1979 by Governor Clinton for high school students. According to the Arkansas Department of Education description, the school "is a five week summer residential program for rising high school seniors. . . . The purpose of the Governor's School is to provide gifted students a challenging opportunity to experience a variety of 20th century theories for the interpretation of facts. The emphasis of the school is on conceptual or abstract intelligence in contrast to practical or concrete intelligence."[6]

Predictably, none of the "20th century theories" presented to the students includes, or even allows, traditional approaches to the arts, the social sciences, the natural sciences, or literature. These "theories" are presented in a value-free context, with students taught that a particular work of art or literature, "has no point—it can be interpreted in many different ways."[7]

Past Governor's School presentations include: a course on "The History of the Role of Women in Society," which taught that pre-historic societies were matriarchies, that "the word 'family' comes from a Latin word meaning 'domestic slave' — woman was merely an incubator," and that "Christianity was anti-woman and anti-sexuality"; a speech that says "a scientist in the truest sense of the word can't be religious"; and a lecture from Hillary Clinton, who explained why she "trusts 'big government' over 'big business.'"[8]

A radical agenda persists today at the Governor's

School. Peter LaBarbera reports in *Human Events* that the 1991 curriculum included:

- a talk from Dr. Mary Daly, a feminist theologian from Boston College, on "Re-Calling the Courage to Sail: the Voyage of a Radical Feminist Philosopher Pirate."
- an essay by Emily Culpepper, a self-proclaimed "freethinking witch," who says Jesus's teachings were "inescapably hierarchical"; that His death upon the Cross was "necrophilic and sadomasochistic"; and that Christianity is "compost."
- a lesson on animal rights given by a representative from the People for the Ethical Treatment of Animals (PETA), a group whose leader has compared chicken harvesting to the Holocaust.
- a lecture from Sarah Weddington, the attorney who defended "Jane Roe" in the *Roe v. Wade* case.[9]

The Governor's School, with its single-minded, politically-left agenda, clearly stifles free thinking and fails to cultivate virtue.

Governor's School director Bruce Haggard explains that he offers no divergent views in the program because "many of Arkansas's brightest young minds were being held back by religious, conservative, overbearing training at home and this is our first shot at them."[10]

But Bill Clinton described the Governor's School as his "dream come true."[11] Students, however, complained that "anyone who disagreed with the teacher's viewpoint was subject to ridicule."[12] And parents were disturbed by this effort to push an agenda on their children.

Any federal educational programs pursued by Hillary and Bill Clinton should be examined in light of the education swindle they pulled off in Arkansas, where their underachieving, expensive, "politically correct" program passed as good "reform."

1. *Laboratories of Democracy* by David Osborne, Chapter 3.
2. Margie Powell's Comments at June 15, 1990. Arkansas Gay and Lesbian Task Force, Little Rock, Arkansas.
3. "An Overview of the Governor's School," Dan Pilkington, Arkansas Department of Education, September 24, 1980.
4. "A Review of the Arkansas Governor's School for the Gifted and Talented 1980", Eddie Madden.
5. *ibid.*, pages 26–27.
6. *ibid.*, pages 23–26.
7. *ibid.*, pages 24.
8. *ibid.*,"Religious Apartheid in Arkansas", Mark Lowery, page 2 in Foundations, Vol.I, Issue 2/3, Summer/Fall 1990.
9. *Human Events,* September 12, 1992.
10. "Religious Apartheid in Arkansas", Mark Lowery, page 2 in Foundations, Vol.I, Issue 2/3, Summer/Fall 1990.
11. "A Review of the Arkansas Governor's School for the Gifted and Talented 1980", Eddie Madden.
12. *ibid.*, page 21.

# Conflicts of Interest
# in Arkansas

*"Everybody in this state is associated."*[1]
— BETSEY WRIGHT
TOP CLINTON AIDE

Arkansas is a small state; politicians, lawyers, businessmen, and other leaders tend to be very cozy.

But a president cannot operate by the lax ethical standards customary to Arkansas politics. As president, Bill Clinton cannot continue the kind of behavior that characterized his Arkansas governorship. As governor, Bill Clinton:

- took campaign contributions from a bond dealer—subsequently convicted of cocaine dealing—who later received millions of dollars worth of state contracts;
- was involved in a questionable business arrangement with the head of a savings and loan that subsequently went bankrupt;
- signed tough ethics laws for state legislators while insisting that both he and Hillary Clinton be exempted from those standards; and
- protected an Arkansas state medical examiner who absolved Virginia Dwire (Bill Clinton's mother) from wrongdoing in a controversial medical case.

## THE LASATER AFFAIR

By 1984, Bill Clinton's half-brother Roger was a troubled drug addict. According to Jerry Seper of the *Washington Times,* in a transcript of an FBI tape presented to a grand jury, Roger Clinton bragged that he took cocaine 12 times a day and routinely took women to the governor's mansion to have sex. The transcript also reported that Roger Clinton bragged that he could buy a quarter-pound of cocaine for $10,000.

Roger Clinton was convicted in January 1985 of cocaine distribution and conspiracy to distribute cocaine as the result of a sting operation. Roger Clinton served one year of a two-year jail sentence, and he now works for Harry Thomason and Linda Bloodworth-Thomason, long-time Clinton allies who produce the television comedies "Designing Women" and "Evening Shade."

But at the time of his arrest, Roger Clinton was working for Dan Lasater, a wealthy investment banker who was a major campaign contributor to Bill Clinton's first three races for governor. According to the *Los Angeles Times,* the Drug Enforcement Administration had suspected Mr. Lasater of being a major cocaine dealer as early as 1983. "State and federal documents describe widespread cocaine use among Lasater, his employees, business associates and friends," the *Los Angeles Times* reported last March. "They cite parties at which vials of cocaine were distributed as party favors, ashtrays filled with the white powder were arrayed among the hors d'oeuvres, and cocaine was served aboard corporate jets."[2]

In May 1985, four months after Roger Clinton's conviction, Mr. Lasater's investment firm, Lasater & Co., received a $750,000 commission from the sale of $30.7 million in bonds for a new state police radio system.

The *Los Angeles Times* quoted a sworn statement that George E. (Butch) Locke, a former state legislator who was an executive vice president of Lasater & Company, made to the FBI. According to the *Los Angeles Times,* Mr. Locke told the FBI that "because Lasater & Co. backed the right individual in Governor Clinton, Lasater & Co. received the contract."[3]

Governor Frank White says that Colonel Tommy Goodwin, head of the Arkansas State Police, informed him in 1983 that Mr. Lasater and Roger Clinton were both under investigation for their illicit drug use. "Bill Clinton had to know about the Lasater investigation as early as 1983," Mr. White told the *Washington Times*. "Too many people knew about it for him to be totally unaware. It's just not possible."[4]

But the Clinton campaign possessed a marvelous power to motivate people to change their minds after talking to the press. Within two days after the *Los Angeles Times* broke its story, the Clinton campaign brandished sworn statements from most of the people quoted in the *Times* either denying the quotes, or saying that they couldn't remember the conversations the *Los Angeles Times* quoted. [Using sworn affidavits to contradict earlier evidence is a deflection device commonly used by Bill Clinton. The transcript of the Gennifer Flowers tapes (see Appendix I) reveals, for example, Mr. Clinton's suggestion that affidavits be used to cover up their affair.]

Colonel Goodwin said that he did not begin an investigation of Mr. Lasater until 1986. George E. (Butch) Locke said that his heavy cocaine use (for which he was subsequently convicted) made him "so stressed and beleaguered that I have no specific recollection of any such statement." Top Clinton aide Betsey Wright said that the whole story was part of a plot by a brilliant mastermind to portray her boss as "some kind of sex, drug, and money-laundering fiend."[5]

The official campaign line was that Mr. Clinton did not know of Mr. Lasater's cocaine use until August, 1986—a year after the bonds for the state police radio system were issued. Governor Clinton stated in his 1986 re-election bid that he never asked Mr. Lasater about his cocaine use during the occasions in which the governor flew in Mr. Lasater's corporate jet. (Mr. Lasater was convicted in 1986 for distributing cocaine to his friends on about 200 "special occasions." He spent four months in a halfway house and two months under house arrest.)

Bill Clinton's account of these events raises serious questions. Was Governor Clinton unaware that a major campaign contributor—in fact, his brother's employer—was a cocaine user? Did he never wonder where his brother obtained the cocaine necessary to fuel his massive habit? Did no one who attended Mr. Lasater's lavish, cocaine-laden parties ever warn the Governor that something was amiss? And why did Governor Clinton wait until a week after his re-election to a fifth term to give Mr. Lasater a state pardon?

## THE ETHICS LAW

During the 1987–88 term of the Arkansas state legislature, Arkansas's first conflict-of-interest law was introduced. The debate over the bill was so heated that the legislature had to be called into special session until the bill passed.

At first, the legislature decided to include all elected officials in the bill. But, as the *New York Times* reported, Governor Clinton led the effort to make sure that the ethics bill only applied to state legislators. "The deletion of the provision that could have covered Mr. Clinton and his wife, Hillary," the *Times* said, "occurred during a private drafting process. The participants included Mr. Clinton, close political aides and allies of the governor, and a senior partner in Hillary Clinton's law firm named Webb Hubbell."[6]

As originally constituted, the bill would have included all public officials. But in June 1987, Governor Clinton wrote to Webb Hubbell—a man whom Mr. Clinton has publicly identified as one of his best friends—asking him to launch a task force to create an ethics code for the state. "Your responsibilities include not only the development of a code of ethics for government in our state but you should also design the best means of adoption of its various components . . . You have the opportunity to design a way in which unethical conduct can be eradicated, along with any vulnerabilities from which we need protection."[7]

In February 1988, the Arkansas House of Representatives passed the ethics code, which then stalled in the Senate. When the bill got to Governor Clinton's office, the provision requiring the disclosure of conflict-of-interests for all "public servants" was eliminated. In fact, the bill's text was cut substantially: it entered the Governor's office with 24 single-spaced pages, and left with 12 double-spaced pages. When it came out of Governor Clinton's office, it required only state legislators to comply with the ethics law. All other public officials in the state—including Hillary and Bill Clinton, county officials, mayors, and people who served on commissions—were not required to fill out ethics forms.

Bill Clinton maintains that he went "far beyond what state law requires" in disclosing potential conflicts of interest. Indeed, this is true, because the state law he signed required him to disclose very little information.

Hillary Clinton said that she did no business with firms that represented themselves before the state, and that she voluntarily refused to accept the percentage of income (which she says is 2-3 percent) that results from business that her employer, the Rose Law Firm, did with the state. Voters had to trust Ms. Clinton on this, since she did not have to comply with any conflict-of-interest law.[8] And even while she contended that she didn't personally work on state business, there was certainly an appearance that she worked as a rainmaker, bringing state contracts through the door of the Rose Law Firm.

Finally, voters can only speculate about the ethics of Hillary Clinton having served as director of major corporations such as TCBY and Wal-Mart, where she exercised considerable power. Did Ms. Clinton really avoid all discussions at board meetings about dealings with the Arkansas state government? Did she make sure that her dealings with these firms were above suspicion?

These serious questions were never answered because of the conflict-of-interest exemption.

## THE WHITEWATER AFFAIR

In 1978, before Bill Clinton was elected governor, he entered into a partnership with James McDougal, a long-time friend whom he met when they both worked for Senator J. William Fulbright in the late 1960s. They formed a corporation, known as "Whitewater Development," which purchased 200 acres of land to be developed as vacation homes. The Clintons owned half of Whitewater Development, but apparently put little money into the venture.

When Mr. Clinton became governor in 1979, Mr. McDougal served as his director of economic development. After Governor Clinton's 1980 defeat, Mr. Mc-

Dougal went into private business and purchased a controlling interest in the Madison Guaranty Savings and Loan in 1982. Meanwhile, the Whitewater Development venture continued. A model house on a lot was built; records show that it was given to Hillary Clinton. Hillary Clinton then borrowed $30,000 from Madison Guaranty to pay for the model house and lot. Whitewater Development continued to make payments on this Hillary Clinton loan through 1985.

At the same time, Madison Guaranty began experiencing financial trouble, and one of the accounts that caused the trouble was Whitewater Development. Whitewater's checking account was constantly overdrawn, and Madison Guaranty paid the Whitewater overdrafts. In 1984, Madison Guaranty hired one of the best law firms in the state—the Rose Law Firm. According to the *Washington Times*, Madison Guaranty paid Rose Law Firm $2,000 a month for 15 months to represent them in its financial troubles. Hillary Clinton has denied that this money was paid to her directly, although she must have received at least a share of the profits, since all fees paid to the Rose Law Firm are divided evenly among the firm's partners. (Generally, in a law firm, the partner who brings business to the firm receives a higher share.)

In January 1985, Governor Clinton appointed as his new securities commissioner Beverly Bassett Schaffer, a lawyer who previously represented Madison Guaranty. Mr. McDougal told the *New York Times* that he had urged Governor Clinton to hire Ms. Schaffer, claiming that "it was to our advantage" that she be hired.[9]

Although Madison Guaranty was near bankruptcy in 1985, Arkansas state officials permitted it to stay open. And Ms. Schaffer defended their actions saying the bank got "no preferential treatment." Hillary Clinton wrote to

Ms. Schaffer urging her to accept a plan for Madison Guaranty to raise capital. The plan was approved, but it was too late: Mr. McDougal was ousted, and Madison Guaranty was seized by federal regulators in 1986.

*Arkansas Democrat-Gazette* columnist John R. Starr observes that the questions raised by the Whitewater affair are very serious, since the evidence suggests that Mr. Clinton may have used his office to enrich himself. "Bill Clinton's answers to questions about his land deal with Jim McDougal are less than satisfying," Mr. Starr wrote. "If what the *New York Times* reported is true—and there are plenty of indications that it is—Clinton's presidential candidacy could be and should be irreparably damaged."[10]

## THE DWIRE AFFAIR

In 1981, Susie Deer, age 17, traveled with her friends to Hot Springs, Arkansas for a night on the town. After getting drunk, they went to a black section of Hot Springs and uttered racial epithets at black residents. One of the residents, Billy Ray Washington, age 22, proceeded to pick up a slab of concrete and throw it through the car in which Ms. Deer was traveling, smashing her mouth and nose.

Ms. Deer went to the emergency room at Ouchita Memorial Hospital in Hot Springs for help. The operation was not dangerous: plastic surgery to the nose and jaw. Three hours into surgery the doctors wanted the breathing tube, supplying air to Ms. Deer's lungs, moved from her nose to her throat. The nurse-anesthetist on duty was unable to do so, and after repeated tries, she finally asked a doctor to do it. By the time the doctor succeeded, Ms. Deer's heart had stopped, and she died.

Nurses and doctors in the hospital knew that this nurse-anesthetist had occasionally slipped on duty. They complained to the Arkansas state medical examiner, Dr.

Fahmy Malak, that her performance in the Deer operation should be investigated. Dr. Malak declared, however, that Ms. Deer was a victim of homicide and based on this ruling, Billy Ray Washington subsequently served six months in prison.

But the nurse in question was not an ordinary nurse; she was, in fact, Virginia Dwire, now Virginia Kelly—Bill Clinton's mother.

Dr. Malak later denied knowing the nurse-anesthetist involved was Bill Clinton's mother, even though an aide delivering the body says he told Dr. Malak there was a question about what happened in the operating room and that the nurse involved was Bill Clinton's mother.

Dateline NBC producer Mark Hosenball reported in *The New Republic* that over a period of five years, "Malak had been challenged in court at least seventeen times by other pathologists; the National Association of Medical Examiners says this is an unusually high figure."[11] Some families even formed a pressure group—Victims of Malak's Incredible Testimony (VOMIT)—to demand that Dr. Malak be fired.

But Governor Clinton not only ignored VOMIT's complaints—he raised Dr. Malak's salary, giving him the second-biggest salary in state government. Only in September 1991 did Governor Clinton suggest that Dr. Malak be evaluated. He was subsequently transferred and became a monitor of venereal diseases for the Arkansas Health Department, a $70,000 a year post.

Bill Clinton has denied using his influence to help clear his mother in complicity in Susie Deer's death. But his denial has changed over time. In a March 1991 interview with the *Arkansas Gazette,* Governor Clinton categorically denied ever speaking with either Dr. Malek, or his mother, concerning the death of Susie Deer. But in a July 1992 statement, Clinton aide Betsey Wright told NBC that Governor Clinton did not "represent" his mother "in the case of Susie Deer. Nor does he recall 'interceding' with Dr. Malak." But Mr. Clinton no longer denies talking with his mother about the Deer case.

Virginia Dwire's story has also changed over time. In an interview with a Hope, Arkansas weekly newspaper she denied ever speaking with her son about the Deer case. But in a 1983 case in which Ouachita Memorial Hospital sued Ms. Dwire, (one in which, according to Mr. Hosenball, she admitted "that she often read the racing form and filed her nails while administering anesthesia"), she testified that she had talked to her son about the case. She did not, however, give any information about the nature or extent of the conversations because her lawyer invoked attorney-client privilege.

It seems, then, that both Bill Clinton and Virginia Dwire have made statements that they never discussed the case with each other. Both Bill Clinton and Virginia Dwire have also made statements that they *have* discussed the case with each other. Bill Clinton denies that he served his mother in any legal capacity, yet her lawyer has invoked attorney-client privilege to protect the conversations that supposedly never took place.

Many questions remain about Susie Deer's death. But Mr. Hosenball argues that Ms. Dwire did talk to her son, Bill Clinton, about the Deer case. "But why, then, would her son vehemently deny any such conversation?" Mr. Hosenball asks. "He wouldn't. Unless, of course, he felt he had something else to hide."[12]

# THE ARKANSAS DEVELOPMENT FINANCE AUTHORITY

One of Bill Clinton's campaign themes was the need for more "investment" in America. If government invests wisely in businesses, Mr. Clinton believes, then more jobs will be created and all Americans will benefit. "The only way to lay the foundation for renewed American prosperity is to spur both public and private investment," says the 1992 Democratic platform.[13] But Bill Clinton's record on such "investments" in Arkansas shows that such programs could easily become national boondoggles.

In 1985, Governor Clinton created the Arkansas Development Finance Authority (ADFA) to create jobs and stimulate the state's economy. But a *Washington Times* investigation shows that ADFA did a surprisingly poor job creating jobs. In seven years, ADFA created 2,751 jobs. Each job cost the taxpayer $13,202 to create—although the average salary was only $15,000.

In many cases, these ADFA contracts were deals worked through the Rose Law Firm.

Park-On-Meter received a $2.75 million ADFA bond issue in 1985; the son-in-law of Park-On-Meter president Seth Ward, Jr. is Webb Hubbell, a Rose Law Firm partner whom Governor Clinton subsequently named to the Arkansas State Supreme Court.

Recipients of ADFA loans also gave the Clinton campaign large contributions. As reported by the *Washington Times* and the *Los Angeles Times*, the biggest beneficiary of ADFA bond underwriting is Stephens Inc., a large investment firm, which received $3.8 million in fees from the state to underwrite ADFA bonds between 1985 and 1991. Stephens Inc. president Warren Stephens raised $50,000 for Bill Clinton's 1990 gubernatorial race and at least $100,000 for his 1992 presidential bid. Mr. Stephens also loaned the Clinton gubernatorial campaign $10,000 in 1990, after receiving a request from the Governor the Friday before the Tuesday election. In addition, the Worthen National Bank, which is 38 percent owned by Stephens Inc., has given the Clinton campaign a $2 million line of credit, and loaned them up to $4 million at one point during the campaign. Arkansas Freightways, a trucking firm in which Stephens Inc. held a big investment, received a $9.6 million bond issue from ADFA in 1989.[14]

In the 1990 gubernatorial race, the *Los Angeles Times* reported, beneficiaries of ADFA business contributed $400,300 to the Clinton campaign—nearly 20 percent of the total amount Bill Clinton raised to fend off Sheffield Nelson.[15]

Roy P. Drew, a Little Rock investment banker and former Stephens Inc. employee, told the *Washington Times* that ADFA was "welfare for the rich" and was Bill Clinton's "own political piggy bank."

1. *Washington Post*, July 12, 1992.
2. *Los Angeles Times*, March 23, 1992.
3. *ibid.*
4. *Washington Times*, March 25, 1992.
5. *Arkansas Democrat Gazette*, March 25, 1992.
6. *New York Times*, March 27, 1992.
7. Bill Clinton letter to Webb Hubbell, June 11, 1987.
8. *New York Times*, March 27, 1992.
9. *Arkansas Democrat Gazette*, March 8, 1992.
10. *Arkansas Democrat Gazette*, March 10, 1992.
11. *The New Republic*, August 3, 1992.
12. *ibid.*
13. *Congressional Quarterly*, July 18, 1992.
14. *Los Angeles Times*, June 28, 1992.
15. *ibid.*

# First Feminist:
# Hillary Rodham Clinton

*"If you vote for my husband, you get me; it's a two-for-one, blue-plate special."*[1]

—HILLARY RODHAM CLINTON

*"I'm not interested in attending a lot of funerals around the world. I want maneuverability. . . . I want to get deeply involved in solving problems."*[2]

—HILLARY RODHAM CLINTON

Hillary Rodham Clinton is a pacesetter in American politics, and she certainly exercises great influence on her husband's political decisions.

Nonetheless, when people attacked Hillary Clinton's ideas during the presidential race, the Clinton campaign became very defensive. They implied that any examination of Ms. Clinton's record is unfair. But, as Katherine Boo observes in *The Washington Monthly*, spouses of politicians should not be exempt from public scrutiny. Ms. Boo contrasts the relatively soft treatment the press has given Hillary Clinton to the hardball investigations of 1984 Democratic vice-presidential nominee Geraldine Ferraro's husband, John Zaccaro: "We have a need to look closely at what Hillary Clinton's firm earns in state business," Ms. Boo writes. "That's a principle easily grasped when the subject is Billy Carter or Armand D'Amato. But in our sympathy for the difficulties women face in the working world, we've allowed relevant questions about wives' careers to be silenced by social mores and public disclosure loopholes John Zaccaro would have cherished."[3]

Americans should be aware of Hillary Clinton's track record. She was an active radical during the 1960s, when she formed friendships with other student radicals who have now become key Clinton advisers. In the 1970s, the then-Ms. Rodham wrote several articles that suggested children should be free to sue their parents, and implied that parental authority over children was similar to slave masters over slaves, or government over American Indians. She has never repudiated these views.

In the 1980s, Hillary Clinton was Chairman of the New World Foundation, where she authorized grants to organizations that backed the Palestine Liberation Organization and the Sandinistas.

Ms. Clinton is extremely ambitious. Early in the 1992 campaign, rumors circulated that she might be a future attorney general, or even an "unelected co-president." "If I get elected president," Bill Clinton told *Vanity Fair*'s Gail Sheehy, "it will be an unprecedented partnership, far more than Franklin Roosevelt and Eleanor. They were two great people, but on different tracks. If I get elected, we'll do things together like we always have."[4]

Whether or not Bill Clinton has remained a New Leftist or is just another liberal is a subject for debate. But there's no debate over Hillary Rodham Clinton's radicalism—she is the first 1960's student revolutionary to live in the White House.

For, as reporter Daniel Wattenberg observes, Hillary Clinton represents the most left-wing faction of the Democratic party. "The image of Mrs. Clinton that has crystallized in the public consciousness," writes Mr. Wattenberg, "is, of course, that of Lady Macbeth: consuming ambition, inflexibility of purpose, domination of a pliable husband, and an unsettling lack of tender human feeling, along with the affluent feminist's contempt for traditional female roles."[5]

Hillary Clinton was not always a liberal. Hailing from Park Ridge, Illinois, Hillary Rodham was, by all accounts, a conservative and an enthusiastic supporter of Barry Goldwater.

But when she went to Wellesley College, Hillary Rodham moved sharply to the left. She was briefly a supporter of Nelson Rockefeller, but then campaigned hard for Eugene McCarthy in the 1968 presidential primaries.

Hillary Rodham was student body president at Wellesley, and she used that position to begin friendships with student body presidents at other prestigious universities. These friendships still last. *The New Republic*'s Morton Kondracke notes that left-wing economists Robert Reich and Ira Magaziner knew Hillary Rodham "as college student body presidents in 1968 and 1969 (at, respectively, Dartmouth, Brown, and Wellesley). Bill Clinton, Mr. Reich, and Mr. Magaziner were students at Oxford together. The four comprise a cozy little group and have been talking to each other about economics, industrial policy, politics, and education for twenty-four years."[6]

When Hillary Rodham was graduated from Wellesley in 1969, she gave the commencement address. "Words have a funny way of tripping our minds on the way to our tongues," she said. "But there are necessary means even in this multi-media age for attempting to come to grips with some of the inarticulate, maybe inarticulable things that we're feeling."[7]

"What does it mean to hear that 13.3 percent of the

people in this country are below the poverty line?" she asked. "That's a percentage. We're not interested in social reconstruction; it's human reconstruction . . . There are some things we feel, feelings that our prevailing, acquisitive and competitive corporate life, including tragically the universities, is not the way of life for us. We're searching for more immediate, ecstatic, and penetrating modes of living."[8] Her commencement address received national attention, and earned her a picture in *LIFE* magazine.

Hillary Rodham and Bill Clinton attended Yale Law School together. Gail Sheehy writes that Bill Clinton, at the time a "sunny southerner with Elvis sideburns," met Hillary Rodham in the library. Mr. Clinton spent the next few weeks poised at one end of the library, Ms. Rodham at the other. Then, one night, Ms. Rodham marched across the library and stood face-to-face with Bill Clinton: "Look, if you're going to keep staring at me, then I'm going to keep looking back," she said. "And I think we ought to know each other's names. I'm Hillary Rodham."[9]

"I was dumbstruck," Bill Clinton recalled. "I couldn't think of my name."[10]

Then the romance began. Ms. Rodham was attracted to Bill Clinton because "he wasn't afraid of me."[11] Bill Clinton knew that his future was in Arkansas, and he took Hillary Rodham there several times—showing off the state's watermelons and introducing her to barbecue and fried pie.

Ms. Clinton began her writing career as an editor of the *Yale Review of Law and Social Action,* a radical publication affiliated with Yale Law School. One double issue she helped edit was largely devoted to a series of Black Panther murder trials taking place in New Haven. Policemen were depicted as pigs in several drawings. "In one," Daniel Wattenberg reported, "rifle-toting, hairy-snouted pigs with nasal drip march in formation emitting 'oinks' and thinking to themselves, 'niggers, niggers, niggers . . .' Another shows a decapitated and dismembered pig squealing in agony. It is captioned, 'Seize the Time!' "[12]

Another article Ms. Rodham helped edit called for radicals to move to a lightly-populated state and seize control. "Experimentation with drugs, sex, individual lifestyles or radical rhetoric is an insufficient alternative. Total experimentation is necessary. New ideas and values must be taken out of heads and transformed into reality." According to Mr. Wattenberg, Hillary Rodham's response to that article was that it was "long on rhetoric, short on action."[13]

Ms. Rodham was soon publishing her own articles, and specialized in an area of law known as "children's rights." A 1977 review in the *Yale Law Journal* describes some of Hillary Clinton's views. Governments engage in risky activities all the time, she argues; the state routinely "takes risks of all kinds when they decide to build a nuclear plant or introduce a deadly pesticide or advocate no-fault insurance."[14]

If these risky ventures are routinely undertaken, she reasons, why should government bureaucrats have any qualms about policies that could harm families? "Apparently we share so much apprehension about potential harm to cherished, albeit fantasized, family values that programs for children must demonstrate immediate success or risk extinction, even in the face of subsequent evidence of achievement."[15]

In a 1979 article, Hillary Clinton expanded her views of children's rights. "Family disagreements that result in legal battles are, of course, of a more serious nature," she wrote. "The most recent example of disagreement between parent and child is found in the abortion cases recently decided by the United States Supreme Court. The Court held that a minor child might seek an abortion without her parents' consent and over her parents' objections if a court believed it to be in the child's best interests."[16]

"Decisions about motherhood and abortion, schooling, cosmetic surgery, treatment of venereal disease, or employment, and others where the decision or lack of one will significantly affect the child's future should not be made unilaterally by parents," Hillary Clinton argues. "Children should have a right to be permitted to decide their own future if they are competent."[17]

Hillary Clinton moreover feels that children's ability to sue extends beyond the family. Ms. Clinton suggests that children "might have special standing to question the proliferation of nuclear power or junk food because of the potential impact or at least unpredictable impact on their and their children's future development."[18]

Even liberals worry about Hillary Clinton's militant support for "children's rights." *U.S. News and World Report*'s John Leo observes that Hillary Clinton has a wrong-minded view of the relations between parents and children. In far too many homes, Mr. Leo contends, children are the rulers, not the ruled: "American children are not suffering from too much parental authority, but too little," he writes. "A great many people now understand that the rights approach will exacerbate friction in the home and open the door for lawyers, judges, bureaucrats, and 'the helping professions' to make a further mess of the family . . . This is a brave new world we can do without."[19]

Based on Hillary Clinton's papers alone, it is fair to forecast that as First Lady she will be an advocate for nationalized, heavily-regulated day care programs, and major expansion of other government programs. Her record as First Lady of Arkansas provides an equal basis for this forecast.

When Hillary Rodham moved to Fayetteville, Arkansas, she learned to hide her radicalism. Hillary Rodham and Bill Clinton lived apart for a year before their marriage, but only in response to "local mores."[20] They were married in 1975.

Ms. Clinton was not content to simply be a political wife. She joined the Rose Law Firm, the most powerful and oldest law firm in Arkansas. The month Hillary Clinton made partner, she gave birth to her only child, daughter Chelsea.

Between 1978 and 1981, Ms. Clinton chaired the Legal Services Corporation (LSC), a federally-funded program that, in the name of helping the poor with legal problems, gives hundreds of millions of dollars to the radical left.

While Hillary Clinton was at LSC, the agency used tax dollars to contribute to political campaigns; to hire four lobbyists and clerical support to fight a California tax-cutting initiative; and to wage a successful war to prevent Reagan Administration budget-cutters from abolishing their own LSC jobs.

Hillary Clinton's conduct as LSC chair was the subject of widespread controversy in Arkansas. In 1980, Senator David Pryor (D-Arkansas) and Rep. Ed Bethune (R-Arkansas) wrote a letter complaining that the Legal Services Corporation had moved beyond its mission of helping the poor to engaging in radical activism.[21]

Another major point of controversy for the Clintons was Hillary's retention of her maiden name—a decision most Arkansans disapproved. After Governor Clinton's 1980 failed re-election bid, the couple decided to change their image. They adopted a more conservative appearance. Before 1980, Hillary Clinton was a brunette; after

1980, she became a blonde. She stopped wearing glasses. Hillary now said her last name was "Clinton," not Rodham. The name change, she told *TIME*'s Margaret Carlson, "meant more to them (the voters) than it did to me."[22] (Note: Daniel Wattenberg reports in *The American Spectator* that Hillary Clinton still files a separate tax return under the name "Hillary Rodham.")[23] As First Lady, she has changed her name use once again, this time to Hillary Rodham Clinton.

Until 1992, Ms. Clinton was active in the Children's Defense Fund, a radical organization devoted to expanding government programs for children. And in 1987 and 1988, Hillary Clinton chaired the New World Foundation, an organization that gives grants to the radical left.

What sort of people did Hillary Clinton fund? She gave $15,000 in 1987 to the National Lawyers Guild, founded in the 1930s as a branch of the American Communist Party. She gave $20,000 to the Christic Institute in 1988, a far-left group that claims a "secret team" led by rogue CIA operatives has conspired for 20 years to destroy America.[24]

In two cases, Hillary Clinton backed groups that support communists and terrorists. The New World Foundation during her tenure as chairman gave $5,000 to the CISPES Educational Fund, a group that columnist Morton Kondracke calls "the American support group for El Salvador's communist rebels, the Farabundo Marti National Liberation Front."[25]

Hillary and Bill Clinton are a power couple. According to Bill Clinton's disclosure reports, Hillary Clinton made $105,711 in 1990 and $92,444 in 1989—nearly three times as much as Bill Clinton made as governor of Arkansas, a position that pays $35,000. Fifty-three percent of Americans think that Hillary and Bill Clinton have a "professional relationship" rather than a "real marriage."[26]

One thing is sure: Hillary Clinton has come to Washington to set the town on fire.

But are Americans ready to be scorched?

1. "CBS This Morning," May 1992.
2. *Vanity Fair*, May 1992.
3. *Washington Monthly*, May 1992.
4. *Vanity Fair*, May 1992.
5. *The American Spectator*, August 1992.
6. *The New Republic*, July 27, 1992.
7. *Life*, June 1969.
8. *ibid.*
9. *Vanity Fair*, May 1992.
10. *ibid.*
11. *ibid.*
12. *The American Spectator*, August 1992.
13. *ibid.*
14. *The Yale Law Review*, page 1526.
15. *The Yale Law Review*, pages 1528–1529.
16. *The American Spectator*, August 1992.
17. *ibid.*
18. *ibid.*
19. *Washington Times*, August 25, 1992.
20. *Vanity Fair*, May 1992.
21. *U.S. News and World Report*, April 27, 1992.
22. *Time*, January 27, 1992.
23. *The American Spectator*, August 1992.
24. *ibid.*
25. *ibid.*
26. *Vanity Fair*, May 1992.

# "Bimbo Eruptions"

*"There are two kinds of opposition research. There's the research you do on your opponents, and there's the research you do on yourself. The first kind has gone pretty well. The second may cost us the election."*
—Clinton Aide Betsey Wright

*"If your opponent picks up a hammer at you, you need to pick up a meat ax and cut off his arm."*
—Bill Clinton

Rumors about Bill Clinton's marital infidelities have circulated for years, but it was not until former Arkansas cabaret singer Gennifer Flowers publicly admitted to a twelve-year sexual affair with Bill Clinton that his alleged womanizing became a major issue. The Gennifer Flowers story broke in the tabloid newspaper, *The Star*, and was supported by her transcripts of taped telephone conversations she had had with Bill Clinton.

These conversations, which were subsequently confirmed by Governor Clinton as authentic, include references to Mr. Clinton's campaign and his standing in the polls; political rivals Mario Cuomo and Bob Kerrey; and a break-in at Gennifer Flowers's apartment.

The Gennifer Flowers's tapes reveal Mr. Clinton advising Ms. Flowers: "If they ever hit you with it [the story of their affair] just say 'no' and go on, there's nothing they can do." Mr. Clinton wonders in conversation "if I'm going to be blown out of the water with this."

Mr. Clinton makes nervous laughter when Ms. Flowers refers to his oral sex abilities. Significantly, he makes no attempt to deny her reference. Indeed, readers are cautioned that Appendix E contains sexually explicit material.

Although the Clinton camp had feared that their own candidate's record might "cost us the election," Bill Clinton survived the Gennifer Flowers's storm. One reason for his survival is that, while the major media did pick up the *Star* story, they did not publish the full transcripts of the Bill Clinton-Gennifer Flowers conversations.

"Why the media censorship?" asked the organization Accuracy in Media of the Gennifer Flowers story. Accuracy in Media points to quotes from leading journalists for an explanation: "Truth is," wrote Eleanor Clift in *Newsweek,* "the press is willing to cut Clinton some slack because they like him—and what he has to say."

Steven Stark of the *Boston Globe* agreed: "The question is whether the coverage, as a whole, has become so one-sided that the mainstream press is not giving the public the whole truth. That has clearly happened. Why have so many baby-boom reporters boosted Clinton? In part, it's because they identify strongly with a liberal, semi-hip contemporary who seems to share their values."

In the interest of full disclosure, and as a result of a successful legal battle with Gennifer Flowers, the unexpurgated Bill Clinton–Gennifer Flowers's transcript is published in Appendix E to this book.

In Appendix F, a partial transcript of the July 17, 1992, edition of the "Sally Jesse Raphael Show" is published.

It was on this show, which was largely censored by the national news media, that former Miss Arkansas Sally Perdue discussed her sexual affair with Bill Clinton.

The Clinton campaign never commented on Sally Perdue's allegations.

In response to what senior Clinton aide Betsey Wright described as Bill Clinton's "bimbo eruptions," the campaign hired one of America's most colorful private investigators, Jack Palladino. As the *Washington Post* reported: "The Clinton campaign is conducting a wide-ranging effort to deflect allegations about the Democratic nominee's private life and has retained a San Francisco private investigator and lawyer to discredit stories about women claiming to have had relationships with the Arkansas governor."[1]

Mr. Palladino is a Boalt Hall Law School graduate, and he and his wife are both proteges of Hal Lipset, the famed 1960s San Francisco private investigator who became famous for doing investigations for Charles Garry, the House Counsel of the Black Panthers. The cases they worked on during the 1960s became legends: the defense of leftists Angela Davis, Eldridge Cleaver, Huey Newton, Bobby Seale, the Soledad Brothers, and even the Hell's Angels. They called themselves the "people's detectives."

Jack Palladino has never let his radical facade prevent him from enjoying the high life. He charges clients a standard $200 an hour and up to $2,000 per day for his services.[2] In July 1992 alone, the Bill Clinton for President Committee paid Mr. Palladino $17,828.19[3] (see Appendix G). Because of federal matching funds, some of this money may have come from the taxpayer.

Mr. Palladino is every bit as flashy as his California image suggests. He likes to strut in expensive suits, silk ties that burst with color, and a dramatic black beard. Jack

Palladino is known as the master of the pre-emptive strike. That explains why Bill Clinton uses him.

If one studies Bill Clinton closely, one sees that his method of operation in dealing with critics is always the same. He believes in the pre-emptive strike. He strikes hard and he strikes early. He believes that he will be successful if he gets both the first and the last word.

Trying to silence the Gennifer Flowers controversy, Bill Clinton appeared on "60 Minutes" before the release of Ms. Flowers's tapes and the story in *Star* magazine.

To neutralize the controversy over his draft-dodging, Mr. Clinton released his letter to the ROTC commander at the University of Arkansas, and then attacked "Republican critics" who discussed the controversy he had fueled, even though it later became known that Republicans had nothing to do with it.

That is the Bill Clinton method: he strikes hard and fast, and, if possible, first. It is a method he and Jack Palladino share.

The Clinton campaign's hiring of this high-profile detective "illustrates not only the fierceness with which the Clinton campaign plans to combat rumors about the governor's personal life," wrote Michael Isikoff in the *Washington Post* during the campaign, "but also the peculiar state of presidential politics in 1992."[4]

1. *The Washington Post*, July 26, 1992.
2. *The Washington Post*, July 26, 1992.
3. Federal Election Committee Report, Bill Clinton For President Committee July 1992.
4. *The Washington Post*, July 26, 1992.

# Bill Clinton's
# Brave New America

*"Whoever refuses to obey the general will shall be constrained to do so by the entire body politic, which is only another way of saying that his fellows shall force him to be free."*

—JEAN JACQUES ROUSSEAU
*THE SOCIAL CONTRACT* (1762)

*"While we can't use the "S" word [socialism] too effectively in American politics, we have found that in the greatest tradition of American advertising the word "economic democracy" sells. You can take it door to door like Fuller brushes, and the doors will not be slammed in your face. So I commend it to you, for those who are willing to compromise on the "S" word."*

—DEREK SHEARER, LONG-TIME FRIEND
AND ECONOMIC ADVISOR TO BILL CLINTON
AUTHOR, *THE NEW SOCIAL CONTRACT* (1983)

Bill Clinton began his quest for the 1992 Democratic nomination by stressing economic issues. He trumpeted his own "low tax, high growth" record in Arkansas and promised a tax cut to primary voters in New Hampshire: "I'm Bill Clinton and I believe you deserve more than 30-

second ads or vague promises. That's why I've offered a comprehensive plan to get our economy moving again, to take care of our own people and regain our economic leadership. It starts with a tax cut for the middle class."

Once Mr. Clinton had secured the nomination, however, he had a new message. According to *United Press International* (UPI), "Arkansas Gov. Bill Clinton, a day after capturing the Democratic presidential nomination, said the only way for the federal government to overcome the deficit is with 'a massive tax increase.' Once the middle class tax cut had served its political purpose, Clinton largely quit talking about it."[1]

Bill Clinton's public vision for America is fraught with contradiction between the candidate's rhetoric and claims about his programs, on the one hand, and their actual content, cost, and impact on Americans, on the other.

"I am a Democrat," Mr. Clinton told the Economic Club of Detroit, "who believes in entrepreneurship and encouraging investment, who understands and believes in market economics, who believes in individual choice and hates bureaucracy." This is his rhetoric.

Bill Clinton's proposals, however, embody the same liberalism touted by Jimmy Carter, Walter Mondale, and Michael Dukakis. The conservative-sounding campaign rhetoric hides a commitment to traditional liberal goals—big government, higher taxes, and massive spending programs.

In fact, Mr. Clinton's proposals do more than repeat tired and failed liberal nostrums. Really his goal is the creation of a new government-industrial complex similar to the corporate state established in Italy in the 1930s. In Bill Clinton's America, Washington will dictate the details of daily economic life in an unprecedented way.

Bill Clinton's vision is based on a repudiation of the tax

cuts and the limit to government growth that triggered the economic expansion of the 1980s. His position paper on "corporate responsibility" does not attack the moral squalor in Congress; instead it calls on more power for those in Washington "who put people first":

"We can never again allow the corrupt do-nothing values of the 1980s to mislead us. Never again can we allow Washington to reward those who speculate in paper, instead of those who put people first."[2]

Bill Clinton proposes a new economic system that will discourage "corrupt" private investment initiatives, and replace them with government investment (taxing and spending). His proposals abound in government interventions into the private sector, each with untold impact on the ability of American business to expand and create new jobs for American workers.

Under the Clinton plan, for example, the federal government would have to create a new bureaucracy to determine how much money each worker, manager, and owner of a business should be paid. His proposals would require government bureaucrats to come up with a complex formula to penalize "excessive pay" in the private sector; such "excess" would not be allowed to be included as a legitimate business expense for tax purposes.

Imagine an even more powerful Internal Revenue Service that determines how much of what each American earns is "fair," and how much of our incomes represents "excessive rewards"?

Is this the kind of policy that "puts people first?"

Additional Clinton "investments" include bigger student-loan programs, more job-training programs, and "lifetime learning for every American, from pre-school to college to job training and retraining."

According to a report by the National Center for Policy Analysis (NCPA), Bill Clinton's new taxes would trigger a sharp drop in available credit in the private economy, thus raising the "misery index" to the levels last suffered under President Jimmy Carter, when inflation rates soared to 13.3% and the prime interest rates to higher than 20%.

"Contrary to Mr. Clinton's insistence that his tax and spend economic plan will spark new investment, create good paying jobs and get the economy moving again," the NCPA reports, "the study shows that his principal taxes would end up driving capital, the life blood of business expansion, out of the economy and hurting the very people he professes to want to help."[3]

The NCPA study concludes that Mr. Clinton's plan would result in a minimum of 747,000 lost jobs and possibly more than 2 million lost jobs over the next four years. The study also forecasts a net drop in Gross Domestic Product under the Clinton plan of $173 billion by 1996.

The Clinton campaign promised "expanded federal efforts": from infant education, to retraining defense workers, to establishing a huge federal police force, to training ex-soldiers to be teachers, to providing child care, to overseeing parental child support, to combating global warming. The cost of these efforts is incalculable.

Bill Clinton's vision doesn't put *people* first. It puts *government* first.

At the 1992 Democratic Convention, Governor Clinton was asked by Italian reporter Antonio Socci to explain the "economic miracle" in Arkansas, inviting comparison with the "Massachusetts Miracle" touted by Governor

Mike Dukakis early in his 1988 presidential campaign. The resulting article, which appeared on August 8, 1992, in the Italian Catholic news weekly *Il Sabato,* is entitled "Comrade Bill." The headline reads, "A Rapport Between Clinton and the Left? In 1987 the Governor visited the [communist] co-op of Legga. To learn."

Antonio Socci reports: "His [Clinton's] is the only state that has come out of the shadow of the [economic] crisis. A small economic miracle. A nice credential for the race for the White House. What had been his prescription?"

The article continues with Governor Clinton's response.

" 'I went to Italy to study,' the Governor replied."

"A probable American President in Italy 'in school' to end the economic crisis? Is this a joke?" Mr. Socci wonders.

"I came five years ago to the province of Florence to find out how the cooperatives, the artisan cooperatives, and the micro enterprises function," Mr. Clinton explained to Mr. Socci in the article. "Then I went back to Arkansas and I helped put together about seventy youth cooperatives."

"Don't tell me this [communist cooperatives] is your economic prescription for the [United] States?" Mr. Socci asked Mr. Clinton.

"Absolutely," he responded.[4]

Mr. Socci could hardly believe that an American presidential candidate was an admirer of the Communist Party cooperatives that were so notorious in Italy. So after interviewing Bill Clinton in New York, the enterprising journalist went back to Italy and interviewed the Communist Party members whom Mr. Clinton had visited there in 1987.

One of the Italian Communists, Vincenzo Coli, recounted his introduction of Bill Clinton to several other

Italian leftists. "Be careful," Mr. Coli said at the time, smiling, "these are Communists and Socialists."

"No problem, no problem," answered the Arkansas governor.

Bill Clinton's 1987 experience with the Italian Communists, and the impression they had on him, will not surprise anyone who reads the position papers for the Clinton campaign. His far-reaching call for a government-industrial complex echos the ideas of the Italian left.

Further, it is to his old friend, Derek Shearer, that Bill Clinton turns for advice on economic matters. Mr. Shearer is a leftist ideologue. He has a long history with the Institute for Policy Studies (IPS), a hard-left advocate of socialism and an institutional critic of capitalism. Mr. Shearer was planning commissioner in "The People's Republic of Santa Monica, California," when his wife was mayor in the early 1980s, and he was a favorite of local celebrities Jane Fonda and her then-husband, Tom Hayden.[5]

Significantly, it was Derek Shearer who cautioned his fellow leftists in the 1980s to keep under cover, insisting that they refer to their utopian economic schemes not as socialism, but as "economic democracy."

In a conference organized by Ralph Nader in October 1981, Mr. Shearer explained: "while we can't use the 'S-word' [socialism] too effectively in American politics, we have found that in the greatest tradition of American advertising the word 'economic democracy' sells. You can take it door to door like Fuller brushes, and the doors will not be slammed in your face. So I commend it to you, for those who are willing to compromise on the 'S-word.' "[6]

In 1977, Mr. Shearer praised the Italian Communist Party for its "strong cooperative movement and a number of successful enterprises and newspapers," and especially applauded its "model of city management" in the Bologna, Italy communist cooperatives.[7]

In his 1980 book, *Economic Democracy,* Mr. Shearer calls on fellow leftists to work as "a party within" the Democratic party to ensure the election of a Democratic president, and then take "direct action" to advance the socialist cause.

In the light of his Italian journey and the record of economic advisor Derek Shearer, Bill Clinton's proposals emerge more clearly into focus.

In simple terms, the sum of Bill Clinton's proposals amounts to a federal government takeover of the management of American business. The Clinton campaign promises "power to the people." This promise is reminiscent of the former Soviet Bloc's guarantee of a "people's paradise."

Bill Clinton even calls for the creation of an "Economic Security Council" that would allegedly perform for American industry the same functions that the National Security Council performs for American foreign policy.

Columnist Don Lambro points to at least five new taxes that businesses would pay as a result of Bill Clinton's closure tax "loopholes," an action equivalent to a 7.8% tax hike. For small businesses whose profit margins are lower than 7.8%, that tax hike would mean the difference between staying in business and going broke.[8] (Businesses, unlike the federal government, close when they run out of money!)

Even *Newsweek* magazine recognized the dangers of Bill Clinton's dream of bigger government. "A look at the details is, in a word, terrifying," *Newsweek* reporter Rich Thomas wrote. "Clinton, despite his neoconservative rhetoric, appears from his policy blueprints to be a programmatic liberal. He proposes at least two dozen new tax and spending programs, including national health insurance, welfare reform, national education reform and universal job training. The Clinton campaign hasn't estimated the cost of its national health plan and says the other three programs should total about $20 billion a year. But the real price is almost certainly higher—perhaps as much as $150 billion, including health-care reform."

"Government outlays to pay for such programs would indeed be tremendous," Mr. Thomas wrote. "For example, Clinton would use new taxpayer revenues to create an education fund administered by the National Science Foundation to provide grants for professionals formerly engaged in defense work to master the latest developments in critical civilian technology fields such as biotechnology, synthetic materials, renewable energy resources and environmental clean-up; to target defense cuts to infrastructure investments; to expand federal efforts to develop environmental technology and create the world's most advanced systems to recycle, treat toxic waste, modernize city sewage systems and clean our air and water; to develop new, clean energy sources; to increase investment in civilian high-tech applied R&D and manufacturing technologies as the need for military R&D diminishes to create millions of high-wage jobs and smooth our transition from a defense-based to a commercial economy; to make special conversion loans and grants available to small business defense contractors through the Small Business Administration (SBA); to increase funding for the Export-Import Bank, targeted to assist small businesses in developing export markets; to develop national apprenticeship programs for non-collegebound youth that will pool the expertise of schools, local businesses, and unions."9

But no matter how much money he spends, Bill Clinton cannot please everyone.

For example: when Mr. Clinton spoke to the "Earth Day" gathering of radical environmentalists at Drexel College last April, he said, "My administration . . . [will] seek to raise the average goal for automakers to 40 mpg by the year 2000, 45 mpg by the year 2020."[10] However, in a speech to the Economic Club of Detroit in August, he said, "I want to raise mileage standards, but I don't think it's fair to impose a burden on the American fleet that has bigger cars than foreign competitors do, and I certainly don't think that you can ask anybody to do anything that's technologically impossible."[11]

On the issue of health care the Democratic platform maintains that "all Americans should have universal access to quality, affordable health care—not as a privilege but as a right."[12] But Bill Clinton never addresses the number one reason for the phenomenal cost of health care in the United States: the ineptitude of the federal government. Instead, his position papers attack the health insurance industry, drug companies, "corporate interests," and competition among private insurers.

In addition, Mr. Clinton proposes to expand radically the costs of health care by providing (government) health coverage to all who suffer from AIDS; to establish a "Manhattan Project" program to find a cure for AIDS; to multiply in all 50 states the number of school-based health clinics, each of which would feature "safe sex" programs and abortion counseling; and to remove AIDS as a barrier to immigration by people attempting to come to the United States from overseas.

The Clinton proposals include a strong endorsement of gun control, without any measures designed to increase the security of the victims of violent crimes. And Governor Clinton proposes a 100,000-person federal police force to help "fight crime."

Bill Clinton promises change for America. But is his agenda a true break from the tax-and-spend policies that liberal Democrats have endorsed in the past? Christopher Georges, an editor of the *Washington Monthly* doesn't think so: "39 of the 49 specific proposals in Clinton's national economic strategy are virtually identical to policies proposed in 1988 by Michael S. Dukakis," Mr. Georges reported.

"Mr. Dukakis offered a detailed plan to invest in America's infrastructure, part of which he labeled the Fund to Rebuild America," Mr. Georges continues. "Mr. Clinton gives us a Rebuild America plank, which reiterates almost all of Mr. Dukakis's planks. Point after point, the agendas match. . . . Mr. Clinton even offers a version of Mr. Dukakis's often-mocked proposal to collect $58 billion by going after tax cheats; the main difference is that Mr. Clinton vows to collect $45 billion by going after foreign tax evaders. It should come as little surprise that Mr. Clinton would fill his agenda with reruns. After all, a number of his top domestic policy advisors are the very people who engineered Mr. Dukakis's agenda."

1. *United Press International,* June 3, 1992.
2. Clinton Campaign position papers.
3. *The Washington Times,* August 24, 1992.
4. All citations are from "Compagno Bill," by Antonio Socci; Il Sabato [Italian], August 8, 1992, pp. 22ff.
5. *Wall Street Journal,* September 9, 1992.
6. Quoted in Rael Jean Isaac and Erich Isaac, *The Coercive Utopians: Social Deception by America's Power Players,* page 131.
7. *ibid.* page 213.
8. *Human Events,* August 29, 1992, page 13.
9. *Newsweek,* September 7, 1992.
10. Bill Clinton address at Drexel University, April 22, 1992.
11. Bill Clinton address at Detroit Economic Club, August 22, 1992.
12. *Congressionally Quarterly,* July 18, 1992.

# Bill Clinton's
# Special Interests

*"For the first time in the memory of [gay] activists, the presumptive nominee of a major political party openly appealed for homosexual support. 'What I came here today to tell you in simple terms is, I have a vision and you're part of it.'"*

—BILL CLINTON
QUOTED IN *USA TODAY*
MAY 20, 1992

Bill Clinton promised to fight "the special interests and the privileged few."[1] But he can't. His proposals pander to the most powerful interest groups in America—Big Labor, liability lawyers, teachers, the homosexual lobby, and the feminists—while he is silent on the most conspicuous interest group of all: the "privileged few" of the Democratically-controlled Congress.

In recent years, Congress has exempted itself from most of the laws it has written for all other Americans. Foremost among these laws is the Independent Counsel statute, which has brought so many "special prosecutions" of executive-branch officials.

But there can be no special prosecutor for Congress; thus, when Alan Cranston, Senate Democratic Assistant

Majority Leader, and Don Riegle, Chairman of the Senate Banking Committee, were implicated in the "Keating Five" scandal, all they got was a slap on the wrist from the Senate Ethics Committee.

Not one member of the Democratic Congressional leadership has been prosecuted for the House Bank scandal, which was masterminded by political appointees of that leadership. In fact, Congressman Dan Rostenkowski simply refused to respond to a federal subpoena issued by a grand jury to investigate the House Post Office scandal. He considers himself exempt from such "political" initiatives.

Bill Clinton hid the congressional leadership from public view during the Democratic Convention in New York, and he has not said one word about Congressional corruption. That's because Bill Clinton is a prisoner to those who have ushered him to power.

## UNIONS

One special interest group that will not be asked to share the Clinton burden is big labor. Governor Clinton's campaign brags that he "received the endorsement of the Arkansas AFL-CIO in every gubernatorial campaign he entered." So it comes as no surprise that he received the endorsement of big labor in 1992.

Here are the facts on what Bill Clinton has to say about labor unions.

In the summer of 1991, Governor Clinton, before he needed the endorsement of big labor for his campaign, endorsed the North America Free Trade Act (NAFTA), which would extend to Mexico the free trade zone already established between the United States and Canada. According to the Governor Clinton of June 1991, NAFTA "should be a giant step toward an economic alliance [in] ne Western Hemisphere." At a Georgetown University speech Governor Clinton said, "I supported giving the Administration fast track authority to negotiate a sound and fair free trade agreement with Mexico."

However, Big Labor is against NAFTA because it wants to keep goods produced by American labor unions protected from competition abroad. So, by the time the general election campaign began, Big Labor weighed in and Bill Clinton's position on NAFTA vanished.

AFL-CIO Union boss Lane Kirkland played along. The *Washington Post* reported in September 1992 that Mr. Kirkland, who had endorsed Bill Clinton, "repeatedly refused to be pinned down on what position labor expected on trade in exchange for its endorsement." The story reported that organized labor "does not plan to push Clinton for specific public commitments that might prove politically embarrassing to his candidacy."

But Governor Clinton made specific public commitments to Big Labor anyway. In spite of all his talk about "change," he made sure that labor union activities in political campaigns would be exempt from any new laws designed to reform campaign financing: his position paper promises "that a Clinton administration would not put burdensome reporting requirements on labor union political activities and donations."

When Bill Clinton demands onerous new legislation and strict limits on other organizations, on business, and on individuals, it aims at "fairness." But demanding the same of Big Labor would be "burdensome" for the labor bosses who want to ensure that their liberal pals in Congress are never defeated. Mr. Clinton says nothing about guaranteeing political freedom to hard-working American rank-and-file union members. Big Labor unions want to spend workers' dues supporting political candidates many of the workers oppose, and Bill Clinton will not support the dissenting workers, even though such protection is now required by law.

There's more. Bill Clinton's program promises Big Labor government programs: a mandatory payment by business for worker continuing education; extended unemployment benefits to jobless workers in the event of a recession; and a program to "meet [the federal government's] first obligation—to recruit, train, and maintain the competitiveness of our own work force." Mr. Clinton promised to oppose repeal of the Davis-Bacon Act, which forces local communities to pay the union scale to workers on federally-funded construction projects. This prevents local workers from getting those contracts, while causing the prices of such projects to skyrocket and preventing poor people from getting jobs that are now given to well-connected union members.

Bill Clinton's labor proposal also calls for repeal of Section 14(B) of the Taft-Hartley Bill. This provision allows states to give workers the right to work without being subject to compulsory union membership. It has long been a target of Big Labor as its membership has dwindled. Today the vast majority of American workers, especially those in the most productive and dynamic parts of our economy, have found labor unions do more harm than good. Mr. Clinton's proposal would make it harder for them to exercise their freedom to work as they please.

The Democratic platform also supports "the right of workers to organize and bargain collectively without fear of intimidation or permanent replacement during labor disputes"—thus restoring to union bosses the power to terrorize businesses they lost after President Ronald Reagan dismissed belligerent air traffic-control workers in the 1981 PATCO strike.

## THE HOMOSEXUAL/PRO-ABORTION LOBBY

Under the Clinton plan, homosexuals become not only a protected minority, but a preferred minority. Homosexual balance in employment will take its place along racial balance quotas. Religious landlords will not be able to evict promiscuous homosexuals from rental property, however concerned they are about the impact such behavior might have on families and children in neighboring apartments. Homosexual marriage and adoption will be legalized, and those putting up children for adoption will not be able to prevent their child from being given to homosexual or lesbian "couples" to be raised in that "lifestyle."

Bill Clinton's America sees no difference between families of "homosexual lovers" and the traditional, monogamous, faithful family. In order to enforce his proposals, Mr. Clinton recommends the takeover of traditional family functions by federal government bureaucracies. He expresses little or no support for families trying to care for their own children, for home or church child care, for home schooling or value-based education, for adoption counseling or other alternatives to abortion, or for abstinence-based sex education programs.

In addition, Mr. Clinton has surrendered completely to the pro-abortion feminists who dominate the Democratic Party.

When questioned about his opinion on the controversial "Freedom of Choice Act"—which allows abortion through all nine months of pregnancy—Mr. Clinton said, "I strongly support the 'Freedom of Choice Act' because we need to guarantee that women can make their own reproductive choices." (See Appendix H) Due to the pressure of the Democratic Party's fire-breathing feminists, Mr. Clinton has dropped all opposition to abortion.

He is now embarrassed by his 1986 statement to the Arkansas Right to Life: "I am opposed to abortion and to government funding of abortions." (See Appendix I)

## THE NATIONAL EDUCATION ASSOCIATION

Bill Clinton's union endorsements include the National Education Association, the nation's largest. In July 1992, the NEA enthusiastically endorsed Mr. Clinton at its annual convention. He responded by issuing a premature invitation to NEA President Keith Geiger to come stay in the Lincoln Bedroom.

But as former Secretary of Education Lamar Alexander observed, "in order to get the nomination, [Bill Clinton] had to make the NEA happy, and the NEA only likes people they can control . . . I've lived long enough to know that, when the NEA gives you a good grade, that means you don't stray very far from their agenda."

What is the NEA agenda? At their annual convention, delegates passed motions to:

- block any form of school choice that involves aiding private schools, including selling closed or surplus public schools to private educational groups;
- ban home schooling unless parents receive state licenses and complete NEA-approved education courses;
- require the federal government to institute national health insurance programs;
- establish mandatory educational programs about AIDS;
- require guidance and counseling programs at all levels of the school system, beginning with kindergarten§sure the passage of the Equal Rights Amendment;

- require all school systems to continue to employ people with AIDS;
- require schools to implement suicide prevention programs; and
- require schools to add to existing teenage pregnancy policies programs that "include development of self-esteem and positive self-concepts."

The NEA has a lot of money to spend on political campaigns. In its 1991 fiscal year, the NEA spent $8.5 million out of a total budget of $164.3 on "government relations" (lobbying and electing NEA members to school boards); $4.7 million on "human and civil rights" (lobbying to pass the ERA, quotas, abortion, banning "sexist" words, and so forth) and $7 million on "communications" (public relations). All this funding does not include the millions the NEA spends directly through NEA-PAC, one of the nation's largest political action committees.[2]

The last successful Democratic presidential candidate the NEA endorsed, Jimmy Carter, rewarded the union with the creation of the Department of Education.

## THE LIABILITY LAWYER LOBBY

Bill Clinton refused to disclose the amount of his funding that came from trial lawyers, but it is significant. The *Wall Street Journal* cites the plaintiff lawyer lobby as the interest group that gave more than any other to the Clinton campaign.[3] By July 27, 1992, the *New York Times* could report that lawyers and lobbyists had contributed $2.5 million to the Clinton campaign, by far the most of any group.

As far back as his early days in the Arkansas statehouse, Mr. Clinton has supported the interests of trial lawyers whose lawsuits drive up the cost of virtually every aspect of American life, from having a baby to planning a funeral. Of course, consumers must eventually pay these costs through higher prices, not to mention lost jobs and the loss of products that never come to market because of the prohibitive cost of liability insurance. Trial lawyers receive as much or more than their clients, and they want to keep it that way.

Trial lawyers exert a profound influence on Bill Clinton. On March 25, 1992, Robert Habush, former president of the American Trial Lawyers Association, wrote his fellow lawyers in Wisconsin a letter urging them to contribute to Mr. Clinton. "I happen to know that Bill Clinton is against tort reform of any kind," the letter said. "Accordingly, I urge all of you to write a check to the Clinton for President campaign and forward it to me so that I can batch them and send them on to Little Rock, Arkansas." (See Appendix J) The proof of the pudding? According to *Legal Times,* a Washington D.C.-based legal weekly, "Arkansas is one of the few states not to have passed any significant legislation limiting liability or cutting down costs in tort litigation."[4]

Mr. Habush's view is supported by the lawyers who know Bill Clinton best. Arkansas lawyer David Williams, president of the Arkansas Trial Lawyers Association, wrote a fundraising letter for Bill Clinton on July 10, 1992 (See Appendix K). He reminisced about the classes he had taken from Mr. Clinton in law school. "There have been a lot of us who have been with him from the beginning," Mr. Williams added. "During all this time, I can never remember an occasion where he failed to do the right thing where we trial lawyers were concerned."

"Just look at our record," Mr. Williams wrote. "Arkansas is one of only four states that has survived the insurance industry's propaganda war unscathed. We have

.o tort reform/deform here in Arkansas. In addition, we have been very successful with our own legislative efforts. This success would not have occurred without Bill Clinton."

In 1987, wrote Mr. Williams, when the Clinton administration presented a legislative package which included some basic tort reform features, "We immediately got on the horn to the Governor about this and the tort reform part of the legislative package was pulled. . . . The Governor dropped the tort reform and it has never come back up."

"He's been real good to the trial lawyers," James Bruce McMath, head of the Arkansas Trial Lawyers Association's political action committee, told *Legal Times*. "He had put a couple of small tort-reform measures in one of his legislative packages one year. We went to meet with him on that, and he apologized and worked with us hand in glove the rest of the way."[5]

And the trial lawyers have been "real good" to Bill Clinton where it matters most—in campaign contributions. A recent study sponsored by CNN and the National Library of Money & Politics found that 40 percent of Bill Clinton's campaign contributions came from lawyers—five times more than any other interest group.

In short, the more powerful the special interest and the fatter the cat, the more likely Bill Clinton will be found in their corner.

1. Bill Clinton, Speech to the American Legion, August 25, 1992.
2. *Phyllis Schlafly Report,* August 1992.
3. Paul Gigot, *Wall Street Journal,* September 5, 1992.
4. *Legal Times,* March 23 1992.
5. *ibid.*

# Bill Clinton's Counterfeit Covenant

> *"To make this revolution, we seek a 'New Covenant'
> to repair the damaged bond between the American
> people and their government."*
> —DEMOCRATIC PARTY PLATFORM, 1992

Bill Clinton made religion an issue at the 1992 Democratic Convention, and subsequently attacked his opponents for inserting religion into the presidential debate.

When seen in the light of his record on the character
issue, on education and virtue, on crime, and on taxes,
Bill Clinton's manipulation of religion comes as no surprise.

Bill Clinton chose the "New Covenant" as his campaign's guiding concept. He politicized it. And he rode it
to victory in November 1992.

Bill Clinton did not have to choose a religious theme
for his political campaign this fall. But, given this choice,
his subsequent attacks on the use of religious themes by
his opponents drip with cynicism.

Bill Clinton chose the theme of a "New Covenant" between the American people and their government as the
crowning jewel of his address to the New York convention.
The delegates he addressed cheered homosexual rights,
abortion on demand, the "new age" religion of environ-

mentalism, and the banning of any support for educational choice outside the government school system.

These noisy delegates needed a theme to pull themselves together. With the "New Covenant," Bill Clinton delivered.

When Bill Clinton declared this religious theme in his acceptance speech, none of these radical special-interest groups walked out in protest or disgust; instead, they stood and cheered. Finally, they had found a leader who was willing to create a Gospel that not only *allows* them to continue their chosen pursuits, but actually *encourages* them. Bill Clinton's "New Covenant" gives a seal of approval to varieties of self-indulgence that a few short years ago would have earned universal religious rebuke.

In Bill Clinton the radical secularists have found their apostle. Supporters of homosexuality, abortion, and environmental extremism have good reason to be pleased at his prospects for victory. Mr. Clinton's convention not only celebrated the rejection of traditional family values cherished by most Americans. It put the country on notice that the fundamental institutions of American life are threatened with radical change.

True to form, Mr. Clinton did his best at the convention to give private support to these radical agendas and their advocates, while prohibiting their discussion during prime time. Only the religious ignorance of the secular media prevented uproar over Mr. Clinton's revisionism in New York.

Bill Clinton's call for a "New Covenant" asks Americans to place a faith in the Clinton government that they have heretofore reserved for God. In his imagery, in his deceptive misquotation of Scripture, and in his call to action, Bill Clinton proclaims a Counterfeit Covenant.

This Counterfeit Covenant promises the triumph of the

secular state. It offers Americans the "opportunity" to remove God as man's savior and to replace Him with an all-powerful government. Bill Clinton will not be satisfied with just garnering the *votes* of the American electorate. His Counterfeit Covenant goes further, asking them to replace the love of God with their glorification of, and their dependency on, political power. All as part of a slick campaign gimmick.

Does this "Covenant" deserve support?

Consider what Mr. Clinton is asking Americans to do: with the proclamation of his "New Covenant," Mr. Clinton perverts language properly reserved in our culture for the sacred relationship of man with God. Furthermore, he seizes the language of the New Covenant proclaimed by Jesus Christ, and applies it to his own administration.

In plain English, this is known as "blasphemy."

It is assumed that Mr. Clinton, an honors graduate of the Catholic Georgetown University and a former Rhodes Scholar, knows what he was doing. Indeed, his blasphemy is historic: no president—not Franklin D. Roosevelt with his "New Deal," not Harry S. Truman with his "Fair Deal," not John F. Kennedy with his "New Frontier," not even Lyndon Johnson and his disastrous "Great Society"—has dared so crudely to appropriate religious symbols for their own political crusades.

Consider the tables turned for a moment. Imagine Bill Clinton and the New York Democrats reacting to a call by, say, Ronald Reagan, for a "New Covenant" between Americans and their government. The cries of outrage at the "religious right's" breach of "the wall of separation" would fill the airwaves. But when Bill Clinton appropriates sacred symbols for his own ends, there are no cries of outrage. There are no sermons from the self-anointed.

In announcing his Counterfeit Covenant, Bill Clinton

...as changed Sacred Scripture to meet his purpose. Mr. Clinton's most flagrant appropriation of God's Word for man's glory is this passage from the Gospel according to Bill Clinton: "Scripture says, 'Our eyes have not seen, nor our ears heard, what we can build.' "[1]

The original Scripture profoundly disagrees with Mr. Clinton. In the words penned by St. Paul,

> What no eye has seen, nor ear heard,
> nor the heart of man conceived,
> What God has prepared for those who love him.

> I Corinthians 2:9 (RSV)

Mr. Clinton's gospel not only proclaims the advent of heaven on *earth*—the central theme of secular modernism—but also the promise that "we" can build it. This "we" does not refer to *all* Americans, but only those willing to abandon the true New Covenant proclaimed by Jesus Christ, and embrace the Counterfeit Covenant of politician Bill Clinton under a new, more powerful secular government. What a cruel choice!

And a cynical one as well. Mr. Clinton's religious campaign theme was designed to mimic Ronald Reagan's successful "family values" campaign, which proved so popular among a broad majority of Americans. But behind Mr. Clinton's facade lurk the special interest groups he will have to please as president: homosexual and lesbian rights lobbies; radical feminists; pro-abortionists; labor union bosses; big-union enemies of Christian education; civil-rights extremists who still demand Affirmative Action and Busing; "children's rights" advocates (under the intellectual leadership of Hillary Clinton); radical environmentalists; and, yes, the media and Hollywood "cultural elites."

Without the support of these special-interest group candidate Clinton would not have won the nomination Without their troops and money, he could not have won in November.

What price will they now ask?

Behind the symbol of Mr. Clinton's Counterfeit Covenant lies his constant invocation of "change." We must assume he means change for the *better*. In Christ's New Covenant, change means repentance for one's sins, and a recognition that salvation comes from God. Spiritual change in Christianity, and Judaism, implies leaving evil ways, (sin), and repenting. In experiencing this conversion, the sinner turns away from his old, deformed life, and models himself on Christ, the source of all truth and order.

Contrast this to Bill Clinton's view of "change." The Christian tradition does not ask us to be better, more efficient sinners; it calls on us to put the life of sin behind us, and turn to the true model of virtue, Jesus Christ, and re-form ourselves on Him.

Bill Clinton's Counterfeit Covenant asks us, in the name of "change," to believe in his goodness to use big government, political power, and the federal bureaucracy to reach the same ends. Bill Clinton, through utopian social engineering, will attempt to build his own "City of God" on earth. Bill Clinton believes strongly that government— not God or the family—should plan and control the future of mankind.

Campaigning for president, Bill Clinton invoked the future in order to discourage a look at his past. He invoked "change" to distract voters from his consistently liberal record. And he designed a set of religious slogans to disguise his campaign's attacks on values central to every traditional American faith.

Bill Clinton's call for a secular covenant with Government as the new deity is the closest that an American political party has ever come to calling for the building of a new Tower of Babel. Bear in mind what happened the last time a power-hungry politician tried that.

"There is nothing new under the sun," Scripture says.

1. Bill Clinton's speech to the 1992 Democrat Convention.

# APPENDIX A

*Below is a letter sent by Ron Brown, the Chairman*
*Democratic National Committee, to radio and television s*
*managers across the country in a successful attempt to sit*
*Floyd Brown's advertisement about Bill Clinton.*

**Democratic National Committee**

Ronald H. Brown
Chairman

August 4, 1992

Dear Station Manager:

I am writing you on a matter of great concern to me and, I am
sure, to the vast majority of the American people who want to see
this year's Presidential election determined on the issues rather
than by the smear tactics which have characterized so many recent
elections and have denigrated our political process.

As you may be aware, the Presidential Victory Committee,
headed by Floyd Brown, sought to place an advertisement with the
media inviting the public to call a phone number in Nevada at a
cost of $4.99 and listen to tapes of alleged phone calls between
Gennifer Flowers and Governor Bill Clinton. The ad sought to lure
callers by alluding to sexually explicit material; Floyd Brown
announced that part of the proceeds would represent profits that he
would utilize for further ads. CNN and other news organization
have reported that they have had these tapes reviewed by experts
who have concluded that they appear to have been deliberately
altered in such a way as to substantially distort them.

Further, CBS evening news on July 13 and 14 ran shocking
reports on Floyd Brown's activities, describing him as engaging in
"police state tactics" and making an Arkansas family the "victims
of an unusually brazen dirty tricks operation." These broadcasts
exposed the outrageous harassment by Floyd Brown and his
organization of the family of an Arkansas woman who committed
suicide in 1977, as part of Brown's unsuccessful effort to connect
her to Governor Clinton.

The disgust over Floyd Brown's tactics has cut across the
political spectrum. After the first CBS broadcast ran, the White
House said that President Bush was "very upset" about the report,
and the President himself stated that he would do whatever he could
to stop Floyd Brown from using his name for such "nefarious
purposes." The Bush/Quayle campaign then filed a complaint with
the Federal Election Commission against Floyd Brown and his group.
The Democratic National Committee is also reviewing the
circumstances surrounding Floyd Brown's operations with a view
towards taking appropriate legal action.

430 South Capitol Street, S.E. Washington, D.C. 20003 (202) 863-8000
Paid for by the Democratic National Committee. Contributions to the Democratic National Committee are not tax deductible.
Printed · cycled Paper

Under these circumstances, I think it is fair to say that by running ads produced by Floyd Brown and his associates, your station would contribute to the enhancement and promotion of smear campaigns of the vilest type. In addition, American voters stand to suffer if such ads are aired and their focus is turned from the issues to such sleaze.

These types of tactics are not new for Floyd Brown and those working with him. The organization with which he was associated in 1988 was the group that produced the infamous Willie Horton ads. In fact, according to subsequent news reports, Mr. Brown's organization tricked the media into running the Willie Horton ads by submitting to television stations one format for the ads, and then after acceptance, substituting another format including the picture of Willie Horton. Lee Atwater, President Bush's campaign manager, later apologized for the entire Willie Horton affair.

Floyd Brown is likely to continue his sleaze campaign, and there is no reason why this time his type of scurrilous advertising should see the light of day. In the first place, I am advised that under FCC rules, your station has no obligation whatsoever to run such ads. I am also advised that if you were to run the ads, you may well incur an obligation to run responses on behalf of Governor Clinton. You should also be aware that the ads may well violate the privacy and other rights of other affected persons, such as the family recently hounded by Floyd Brown.

I trust you will agree that our country deserves better in this election than being subjected to another "Willie Horton" campaign, and please accept my personal thanks for whatever you can do to ensure that this does not reoccur.

Sincerely,

Ronald H. Brown
Chairman,
Democratic National Committee

# APPENDIX B

*Below is Bill Clinton's December 1969 letter to his RO\
Director, Colonel Eugene Holmes.*

I am sorry to be so long in writing. I know I promised to let
you hear from me at least once a month, and from now on you
will, but I have had to have some time to think about this first
letter. Almost daily since my return to England I have thought
about writing, about what I want to and ought to say.

First, I want to thank you, not just for saving me from the
draft, but for being so kind and decent to me last summer, when
I was as low as I have ever been. One thing which made the
bond we struck in good faith somewhat palatable to me was my
high regard for you personally. In retrospect, it seems that the
admiration might not have been mutual had you known a little
more about me, about my political beliefs and activities. At
least you might have thought me more fit for the draft than for
ROTC.

Let me try to explain. As you know, I worked for two years
in a very minor position on the Senate Foreign Relations Committee. I did it for the experience and the salary but also for
the opportunity, however small, of working every day against a
war I opposed and despised with a depth of feeling I had reserved solely for racism in America before Vietnam. I did not
take the matter lightly but studied it carefully, and there was a
time when not many people had more information about Vietnam at hand than I did.

I have written and spoken and marched against the war. One
of the national organizers of the Vietnam Moratorium is a close
friend of mine, After I left Arkansas last summer, I went to
Washington to work in the national headquarters of the Moratorium, then to England to organize the Americans for the
demonstrations Oct. 15 and Nov. 16.

Interlocked with the war is the draft issue, which I did not
begin to consider separately until early 1968. For a law seminar

rgetown I wrote a paper on the legal arguments for and
st allowing, within the Selective Service System, the clas-
ation of selective conscientious objection, for those opposed
articipation in a particular war, not simply to "participation
war in any form."

From my work I came to believe that the draft system itself
s illegitimate. No government really rooted in limited, parlia-
mentary democracy should have the power to make its citizens
fight and kill and die in a war they may oppose, a war which
even possibly may be wrong, a war which, in any case, does not
involve immediately the peace and freedom of the nation.

The draft was justified in World War II because the life of
the people collectively was at stake. Individuals had to fight, if
the nation was to survive, for the lives of their countrymen and
their way of life. Vietnam is no such case. Nor was Korea an
example where, in my opinion, certain military action was justified but the draft was not, for the reasons stated above.

Because of my opposition to the draft and the war, I am in
great sympathy with those who are not willing to fight, kill, and
maybe die for their country (i.e. the particular policy of a particular government) right or wrong. Two of my friends at Oxford
are conscientious objectors. I wrote a letter of recommendation
for one of them to his Mississippi draft board, a letter which I
am more proud of than anything else I wrote at Oxford last
year. One of my roommates is a draft resister who is possibly
under indictment and may never be able to go home again. He
is one of the bravest, best men I know. That he is considered a
criminal is an obscenity.

The decision not to be a resister and the related subsequent
decisions were the most difficult of my life. I decided to accept
the draft in spite of my beliefs for one reason: to maintain my
political viability within the system. For years I have worked to
prepare myself for a political life characterized by both practical
political ability and concern for rapid social progress. It is a life
I still feel compelled to try to lead. I do not think our system
of government is by definition corrupt, however dangerous and
inadequate it has been in recent years. (The society may be

corrupt, but that is not the same thing, and if that is
are all finished anyway.)

When the draft came, despite political convictions, I wa
ing a hard time facing the prospect of fighting a war I had
fighting against, and that is why I contacted you. ROTC
the one way left in which I could possibly, but not positive
avoid both Vietnam and resistance. Going on with my educatior
even coming back to England, played no part in my decision tc
join ROTC. I am back here, and would have been at Arkansas
Law School because there is nothing else I can do. In fact, I
would like to have been able to take a year out perhaps to teach
in a small college or work on some community action project
and in the process to decide whether to attend law school or
graduate school and how to begin putting what I have learned
to use.

But the particulars of my personal life are not nearly as important to me as the principles involved. After I signed the
ROTC letter of intent I began to wonder whether the compromise I had made with myself was not more objectionable than
the draft would have been, because I had no interest in the
ROTC program in itself and all I seemed to have done was to
protect myself from physical harm. Also, I began to think I had
deceived you, not by lies because there were none but by failing
to tell you all the things I'm writing now. I doubt that I had the
mental coherence to articulate them then.

At that time, after we had made our agreement and you had
sent my 1-D deferment to my draft board, the anguish and loss
of my self-regard and self confidence really set in. I hardly slept
for weeks and kept going by eating compulsively and reading
until exhaustion brought sleep. Finally, on Sept. 12 I stayed up
all night writing a letter to the chairman of my draft board,
saying basically what is in the preceding paragraph, thanking
him for trying to help in a case where he really couldn't, and
stating that I couldn't do the ROTC after all and would he please
draft me as soon as possible.

I never mailed the letter, but I did carry it on me every day
until I got on the plane to return to England. I didn't mail the

cause I didn't see, in the end, how my going in the army aybe going to Vietnam would achieve anything except a g that I had punished myself and gotten what I deserved.

came back to England to try to make something of this ond year of my Rhodes scholarship.

And that is where I am now, writing to you because you have een good to me and have a right to know what I think and eel. I am writing too in the hope that my telling this one story will help you to understand more clearly how so many fine people have come to find themselves still loving their country but loathing the military, to which you and other good men have devoted years, lifetimes, of the best service you could give. To many of us, it is no longer clear what is service and what is disservice, or if it is clear, the conclusion is likely to be illegal.

Forgive the length of this letter. There was much to say. There is still a lot to be said, but it can wait. Please say hello to Col. Jones for me.

Merry Christmas.

Sincerely,
Bill Clinton

# APPENDIX C

*Below is Colonel Eugene Holmes's September 1992 affic*
*concerning Bill Clinton and the draft.*

*Colonel Eugene Holmes is a highly decorated officer of the Unite*
*States Army. He is a survivor of the Bataan Death March and*
*3½ years as a POW of the Japanese. He served 32 years in the*
*army before retiring with 100% disability. His decorations include*
*the Silver Star, 2 Bronze Stars, 2 Legions of Merit, the Army*
*Commendation Medal and many others. During the Vietnam*
*War, he personally inducted both his sons into the service--one*
*for 3 years as a regular army enlisted man, and the other as a*
*commissioned officer (after he had completed ROTC training).*

There have been many unanswered questions as to the circumstances surrounding Bill Clinton's involvement with the ROTC department at the University of Arkansas. Prior to this time I have not felt the necessity for discussing the details. The reason I have not done so before is that my poor physical health (a consequence of participation in the Battan Death March and the subsequent 3½ years interment in Japanese POW camps) has precluded me from getting into what I felt was unnecessary involvement. However, present polls show that there is the imminent danger to our country of a draft dodger becoming Commander-in-Chief of the Armed Forces of the United States. While it is true, as Mr. Clinton has stated, that there were many others who avoided serving their country in the Vietnam war, they are not aspiring to be the President of the United States.

The tremendous implications of the possibility of his becoming Commander-in-Chief of the United States Armed Forces compels me now to comment on the facts concerning Mr. Clinton's evasion of the draft.

This account would not have been imperative had Bill Clinton been completely honest with the American public concerning this matter. But as Mr. Clinton replied on a news conference

ning (September 5, 1992) after being asked another par-
about his dodging the draft, "Almost everyone con-
d with these incidents are dead. I have no more comments
ake". *Since I may be the only person living who can give a
t hand account of what actually transpired, I am obligated by
y love for my country and my sense of duty to devulge what
ctually happened and make it a matter of record.*

Bill Clinton came to see me at my home in 1969 to discuss
his desire to enroll in the ROTC program at the University of
Arkansas. We engaged in an extensive, approximately two (2)
hour interview. At no time during this long conversation about
his desire to join the program did he inform me of his involvement, participation and actually organizing protests against the
United States involvement in South East Asia. He was shrewed
enough to realize that had I been aware of his activities, he
would not have been accepted into the ROTC program as a
potential officer in the United States Army.

The next day I began to receive phone calls regarding Bill
Clinton's draft status. I was informed by the draft board that it
was of interest to Senator Fullbright's office that Bill Clinton,
a Rhodes Scholar, should be admitted to the ROTC program.
I received several such calls. The general message conveyed by
the draft board to me was that Senator Fullbright's office was
putting pressure on them and that they needed my help. I then
made the necessary arrangements to enroll Mr. Clinton into the
ROTC program at the University of Arkansas.

I was not "saving" him from serving his country, as he er-
roneously thanked me for in his letter from England (dated
December 3, 1969). I was making it possible for a Rhodes
Scholar to serve in the military as an officer.

In retrospect I see that Mr. Clinton had no intention of following through with his agreement to join the Army ROTC
program at the University of Arkansas or to attend the University of Arkansas Law School. I had explained to him the
necessity of enrolling at the University of Arkansas as a student
in order to be eligible to take the ROTC program at the University. He never enrolled at the University of Arkansas, but

instead enrolled at Yale after attending Oxford. *I belie*
*he purposely deceived me, using the possibility of joinir.*
*ROTC as a ploy to work with the draft board to delay h.*
*duction and get a new draft classification.*

The December 3rd letter written to me by Mr. Clinton, a
subsequently taken from the files by Lt. Col. Clint Jones, n.
executive officer, was placed into the ROTC files so that a recorc
would be available in case the applicant should again petition
to enter the ROTC program. The information in that letter alone
would have restricted Bill Clinton from ever qualifying to be an
officer in the United States Military. Even more significant was
his lack of veracity in purposefully defrauding the military by
deceiving me, both in concealing his anti-military activities overseas and his counterfeit intentions for later military service.
These actions cause me to question both his patriotism and his
integrity.

When I consider the calabre, the bravery, and the patriotism
of the fine young soldiers whose deaths I have witnessed, and
others whose funerals I have attended. . . . When I reflect on
not only the willingness but eagerness that so many of them
displayed in their earnest desire to defend and serve their country, it is untenable and incomprehensable to me that a man who
was not merely unwilling to serve his country, but actually protested against its military, should ever be in the position of
Commander-in-Chief of our armed Forces.

I write this declaration not only for the living and future
generations, but for those who fought and died for our country.
If space and time permitted I would include the names of the
ones I knew and fought with, and along with them I would
mention my brother Bob, who was killed during World War II
and is buried in Cambridge, England (at the age of 23, about
the age Bill Clinton was when he was over in England protesting
the war).

I have agonized over whether or not to submit this statement
to the American people. But, I realize that even though I served
my country by being in the military for over 32 years, and having
gone through the ordeal of months of combat under the worst

ditions followed by years of imprisonment by the Japa-
it is not enough. I'm writing these comments to let every-
know that I love my country more than I do my own personal
arity and well-being. I will go to my grave loving these United
ates of America and the liberty for which so many men have
ught and died.

Because of my poor physical condition this will be my final
statement. I will make no further comments to any of the media
regarding this issue.

Eugene J. Holmes
Colonel, U.S.A., Ret.
September 1992

# APPENDIX D

*Below is Gennifer Flowers's statement to the press conc▪*
*her 12-year affair with Governor Bill Clinton.*

Good afternoon. This whole experience is not easy for m▪
I will start by explaining why I came forward to tell my stor▪
about my affair with Governor Bill Clinton. I quite simply was
afraid. Afraid I'd be out on the street without a job. I had
already started to lose singing engagements because of the rumors about Bill and me, and I thought I'd lose my state job Bill
helped me get. The pressure was so intense, I thought I might
have to leave Little Rock, which is my home.

In 1990 Larry Nichols had filed a lawsuit naming me as one
of Bill's lovers. The rumor spread and the pressure was enor-
mous. I was scared and I was alone. To protect myself I began
taping my telephone conversations. The situation was snow-
balling and I didn't know what was going to happen next. I
wanted to have a record of the relationship. Then things got out
of control. First I heard that Star was going to run a story about
Larry Nichols' law suit. When I heard Bill describe our relationship as an absolute, total lie, I knew what my decision should
be. To tell my side of the story truthfully, and as quickly as
possible. So I'm here to repeat, in front of all of you, what I
said in my Star article.

Yes, I was Bill Clinton's lover for twelve years, and for the
past two years I have lied to the press about our relationship to
protect him. The truth is, I loved him. Now he tells me to deny
it. Well, I'm sick of all the deceit, and I'm sick of all the lies.
Last night I sat and watched Bill on 60 Minutes. I felt disgusted
and I saw a side of Bill that I had never seen before. He is
absolutely lying. I'm disappointed, but realistically I never
thought he would come out and admit it. When people hear my
tapes, I think they will realize that I am not a woman that he

poke to infrequently. My tapes go far beyond that,
my tapes go far beyond what Bill described last evening.
cribed our relationship as a friendly acquaintance that
ry limited - friendly, but limited. Listen to the tape ex-
s. Judge for yourself if this is the way a man talks to a
man who is just a friendly acquaintance.

There were two conversations in the tapes that embarrass me
now, but remember, I was talking to a man I had loved for
twelve years. I feel confident about my story because I'm telling
the truth. The man on 60 Minutes was not the man I fell in love
with. I dealt with my hurt for . . . I have dealt with my hurt for
two years now, so this is nothing new to me. I would have liked
to think that after a twelve year relationship he would have had
the guts to say 'Yes, I had an affair with this woman, but it's
over. And that's the truth.' Thank you.

# APPENDIX E

*Below is a transcript of the telephone conversations between Governor Bill Clinton and Ms. Gennifer Flowers between September and December 1991, as released by the Star at a New York press conference in January 1992.*

**FLOWERS.** Are you there? Sorry about that. Mother was . . . wanted me to get her a glass of water. See that was another thing. See, my parents are here, and I'll tell you what, the last thing I needed was to. . . .

**CLINTON.** Have that happen. . . .

**FLOWERS.** . . . . have that happen cause my mother would get very concerned and worried and so far you know. . . .

**CLINTON.** [garbled] If they ever hit you with it just say 'no' and go on, there's nothing they can do.

**FLOWERS.** Well I will, but I mean . . . I. . . . you know . . . she's my mother and you know how mothers can be.

**CLINTON.** They don't want to hear it at all.

**FLOWERS.** Well, she would just get all in a tizzy about. . . . about it and uh, so I thought 'Good God, that's all I need.' Cause they're, uh, they're gonna be here . . . well they're leaving Wednesday morning and they were at the club tonight and they'll be here tomorrow night, which, you know, parents do. And I thought, 'Oh, please Jesus, don't let those people be out there.'

**CLINTON.** I'm just sorry that you ever had to put up with that [next word is garbled].

**FLOWERS.** Well, you know, to be real honest with you, I'm not completely surprised. I didn't think it would start this quickly. But I think, Bill, you're being naive if you think that these other shows like 'Current Affair' and, oh, what are some of the others, uh . . .

**CLINTON.** Well, I thought they. . . .

**FLOWERS.** 'Hard Copy.'

**CLINTON.** I thought they'd look into it. But, you know, I just

a crazy person like Larry Nichols is not enough to get
ry on the television with names in it.

VERS. Right. Well, he better not get on there and start
ming names.

NTON. Well, that's what I mean. You know, if all the
people who are named. . . . deny it . . . That's all, I mean,
I expect them to come look into it and interview you and
everything, uh, but I just think that if everybody's on record
denying it you've got no problem.

FLOWERS. Well, I don't think . . . I don't think it . . . I
don't. . . . Well, why would they waste their money and time
coming down here unless someone showed 'em some interest?
See, they weren't here tonight and they're not going to be
there.

CLINTON. No, no. See, that's it. I mean, they're gonna run
this Larry Nichols thing down, they're gonna try to goad
people up, you know, but if everybody kinda hangs tough,
they're just not going to do anything. They can't.

FLOWERS. No. They can't.

CLINTON. They can't run a story like this unless somebody
said, 'Yeah, I did it with him.'

[apparent end of first segment]

CLINTON. I'll tell you what, it would be extremely valuable
if they ever do run anybody by me, you know. If they ever
get anybody to do this, just to have, like I told you before
when I called you, is to have an on-file affidavit explaining
that, you know, you were approached by a Republican and
asked to do that.

FLOWERS. Mm hmm. Well. . . .

CLINTON. [garbled] . . . the more I think about it, you should
call him back. . . . [garbled]. . . . just don't know.

FLOWERS. Well, I think that . . . Well, are you going to run?
[laughs] Can you tell me that?

CLINTON. I want to. I wonder if I'm going to be blown out
of the water with this. I don't see how they can [garbled word]
so far.

FLOWERS. I don't think they can. . . .

**CLINTON.** If they don't, if they don't have pictures.

**FLOWERS.** Mh hmm.

**CLINTON.** . . . . which they [garbled] . . . anybody a~
one says anything then they don't have anything and arg~
if someone says something, they don't have much.

**FLOWERS.** If they could blow you out of the water they wo~
have already blown you. I really believe that because I belie~
that there are various ones that have been trying hard lately.
See, like that 'Inside Edition.' Uh, there've probably been
other sources too. [Pause] So . . . I don't think so. I honestly
don't. That's my gut feeling. I would tell you if I did. [pause]
But . . . you may know more about. . . .

**CLINTON.** How do you like holding [garbled word]. . . . future in. . . . [garbled word] hands? . . . Do you like that?

**FLOWERS.** Yeah. [laughs] No. Well, if it's positive I do, you
know. I mean cause I want you to . . . I would love to see
you go. . . . Oh, I'd love to see you be President. I think that
would be wonderful. I think you'd make a, a damn good one.
I don't like Bush. I think he's a sneaky bastard. [laughs]
[garbled] He's two-faced. I'd just love to see somebody get
in there for a change, really make a difference. But uh . . . It's
like I told you before, whatever you need me to do, just let
me know.

**CLINTON.** I will.

[Apparent end of tape two]

**FLOWERS.** . . . . remember a long time ago when you called
me and said that if you announced for, well, it was back the
first time you were going to announce for, uh. . . .

**CLINTON.** Governor?

**FLOWERS.** No. President [laughs] [garbled] And you said
[garble] 'Gennifer, just wanted you to know that there might
be some reporters or something out there' and you said, 'Now,
uh, you be sure to [garbled words] [both laugh] say 'there's
nothing to the rumor,' and I said, O. K., I, well I shouldn't
even say this to you, probably embarrass you. Do you remember what I said to you?

**CLINTON.** No. What'd you say?

**ERS.** I said, 'Well, at the time you eat good p*ssy,' [laughs]

**TON.** What?

**WERS.** I said I had to tell them that you ate good p*ssy and you said, 'Well you can tell them that if I don't run for President [laughs]. I've got to keep my voice down, my parents are in the other. . . . [laughs] [garbled]

**CLINTON.** [garbled]

**FLOWERS.** And I thought, you know that's not real funny right now. But anyway I try to find the humor in things.

**CLINTON.** Don't I know it. [garbled] [garbled]

**FLOWERS.** Well, I can guarantee you that's not something I've thought about [laughs], that's not the first thing on my mind when I think about those reporters being down there.

**CLINTON.** God.

**FLOWERS.** Oh, Lord.

**CLINTON.** [garbled]

**FLOWERS.** But, anyway, I think we're o. k. for now.

**CLINTON.** [garbled]. . . . we have to watch as we go along.

**FLOWERS.** Well, you're uh, you know, from the feedback I'm getting around me about various things that are going on with what you're doing, I'm getting very positive feed- back.

**CLINTON.** Yeah, there's no negative except this.

**FLOWERS.** This is the only thing.

**CLINTON.** And there's no negative to me running except this and even if I win . . . as a matter of fact it might be better for me to lose the primary, I might lose the nomination to Bob Kerrey because he's um . . . got all the Gary Hart/ Hollywood money and because he's single, looks like a movie star, won the Medal of Honor, and since he's single, nobody cares if he's screwing. [laughs]

[apparent end of tape three]

[Dial tone]

**[Dialing sounds]**

[Ringing]

**VOICE.** Governor's mansion, Roger Creek.

**FLOWERS.** Is Bill Clinton in please?

**VOICE.** M'am, he's with some people right now. M... who's calling?

**FLOWERS.** This is Gennifer Flowers, I'm returning his...

**VOICE.** Gennifer Fowler?

**FLOWERS.** Flowers.

**VOICE.** O.K. Hang on just a second.

**FLOWERS.** All right.

[long pause]

**CLINTON.** Hello?

**FLOWERS.** Bill?

**CLINTON.** Hey.

**FLOWERS.** It's Gennifer.

**CLINTON.** How ya doin?

**FLOWERS.** Well, I'm fine, it hardly sounds like you.

**CLINTON.** Oh, I'm having terrible throat problems.

**FLOWERS.** [cough] You're making me want to clear my throat. Can you talk? Can you talk a second?

**CLINTON.** Yes.

**FLOWERS.** Uh, I'm sorry I had missed your call. I went up to see my mother for a few days.

**CLINTON.** That's what I figured. How's she doin?

**FLOWERS.** Well, she's, she's doing o. k. physically. . . .

[apparent end of tape four]

**FLOWERS.** Hello?

**CLINTON.** Gennifer?

**FLOWERS.** Yes.

**CLINTON.** It's Bill Clinton.

**FLOWERS.** Hi Bill.

**CLINTON.** Hey I tried to call ya. I can't believe I got ya.

**FLOWERS.** Well whendya try to call me?

**CLINTON.** Last night. Late.

**FLOWERS.** Well I was here.

**CLINTON.** Did you take your phone off the hook?

**FLOWERS.** Well, I did, I. . . . Well, I've been getting these hang-up calls . . .

**CLINTON.** Oh.

**RS.** . . . . and at one point I took my phone . . . I, didn't take it off the hook, I just, uh. . . .

**ON.** Turned it off?

**VERS.** Yeah.

**NTON.** Oh that's what it was. I called . . . I started calling on as I got home last night and I called for a couple of hours.

**LOWERS.** Well, sorry I missed you.

**CLINTON.** [garbled] . . . I was afraid I screwed up the number or something, and I kept calling.

**FLOWERS.** Well are you. . . . you got a cold?

**CLINTON.** Yeah. Oh it's just my . . . every year about this time I . . . My sinuses go bananas.

**FLOWERS.** Yeah, me too.

**CLINTON.** And I've been in this stupid airplane too much, but I'm o. k.

**FLOWERS.** Well, good. Good. The reason I was calling was to tell you that, uh, well, a couple things. Uh, this last Wednesday, someone got into my apartment.

**CLINTON.** Hold on a minute.

**FLOWERS.** O. K.

[long pause]

**CLINTON.** O. k., I got it.

**FLOWERS** Are you in Little Rock?

**CLINTON.** No. . . .

**FLOWERS.** No.

**CLINTON.** I am going to be there tonight late. I'm in, uh, Washington now and. . . .

**FLOWERS.** Well. . . .

**CLINTON.** I'm going to Dallas, and then I'm coming to Little Rock.

**FLOWERS.** Uh, well. . . .

**CLINTON.** So somebody broke in your apartment?

**FLOWERS.** Well, yeah, well . . . There wasn't any sign of a break-in, uh, but the drawers and things . . . There wasn't anything missing that I can tell but somebody had . . .

**CLINTON.** Somebody had gone through all your stuff?

**FLOWERS.** . . . . And gone through my stuff.

**CLINTON.** You think they were . . . But they didn't st
thing?

**FLOWERS.** No. No, my jewelry . . . I had jewelry her
everything, it was still here.

**CLINTON.** You think they were trying to look for someth
on us?

**FLOWERS.** I think so. Well, I mean . . . why, why else
Um . . .

**CLINTON.** You weren't missing any, any kind of papers or
anything?

**FLOWERS.** Well, like what kind of papers?

**CLINTON.** Well I mean did . . . any kind of personal records
or checkbooks or anything like that? . . . Phone records?

**FLOWERS.** Do I have any?

**CLINTON.** Yeah.

**FLOWERS.** Unh unh. I mean, why would I?

**CLINTON.** I don't know I just. . . .

**FLOWERS.** You. . . . you usually call me, for that matter. And
besides, who would know?

**CLINTON.** Isn't that amazing?

**FLOWERS.** Even if I had it on my phone record . . . Oh, well,
I guess they might be able to say 'Oh well, you were in Washington on this date and maybe at that number and connect
that but. . . .

**CLINTON.** Well. . . .

**FLOWERS.** See, you've always called me. So that's not a. . . .

**CLINTON.** I wouldn't care if they. . . . you know, I, I . . .
They may have my phone records on this computer here, but
I don't think it. . . . That doesn't prove anything.

**FLOWERS.** Well, that. . . . that's true. But I just want to tell
you about that.

**CLINTON.** Wow.

**FLOWERS.** Let me tell you something positive.

**CLINTON.** What?

**FLOWERS.** Uh, I heard, uh. . . . I've heard a couple of people
say . . . one had been to San Antonio, the other had been to

ngeles. . . . and they both said that they were, uh, that
ey heard out there was 'Clinton, Clinton, Clinton,'
. .

**TON.** Really?

**WERS.** Yeah. So I thought that was exciting.

**NTON.** We've worked so hard.

**OWERS.** I know you have, but I . . . That may not be a lot, but I mean, that's a . . . I think that's a good indication.

**CLINTON.** Well, no . . . Most people think, you know, that, except for Cuomo, I'm doing the best right now and uh. . . . We're leading in the polls in Florida; . . . without Cuomo in there, but Cuomo's at 87 percent name recognition, and I have 54 percent so. . . . I mean . . . I'm at a terrible disadvantage in name recognition still, but we're coming up, and . . . so I . . . We're moving pretty well, I'm really pleased about it.

**FLOWERS.** Well, I don't particularly care for Cuomo's uh, demeanor.

**CLINTON.** Boy, he is so aggressive.

**FLOWERS.** Well, he seems like he could get real mean [laughs]

**CLINTON.** [garbled]

**FLOWERS.** Yeah. . . . I wouldn't be surprised if he didn't have some mafioso major connections.

**CLINTON.** Well he acts like one [laughs]

**FLOWERS.** Yeah.

[apparent end of tape five]

**FLOWERS.** The only thing that concerns me, where I'm, I'm concerned at this point is the state job.

**CLINTON.** Yeah, I never thought about that, but as long as you say you've just been looking for one, you'da check on it. If they ever ask you if you've talked to me about it, you can say no.

[apparent end of tape six]

**FLOWERS.** Alright, darling, well you hang in there. I don't mean to worry you. I just. . . .

**CLINTON.** [garbled] . . . . I just want to know these things and. . . . if I can help you, you let me know [garbled]

**FLOWERS.** Well, when you can help me is if I de_
to get the heck out of here.

**CLINTON.** All you need to do is let me know. . . .

**FLOWERS.** Because I don't know . . . I don't know w_
turn. I really don't. I mean my contacts have just sort of f_
in Nashville, it's been a long time and, I don't know, I c_
know anybody.

**CLINTON.** [garbled words] . . . . I'll help you.

**FLOWERS.** O. K. Well, I'll, I'll be back in touch, and, uh_
you will let me know if you know anything I need to know
about.

**CLINTON.** I will.

**FLOWERS.** O. K? [laugh]

**CLINTON.** Goodbye, baby.

**FLOWERS.** Talk to you later. Bye.

END OF TRANSCRIPTS--Gennifer Flowers/Bill Clinton

# APPENDIX F

*... is partial transcript of the July 17, 1992 "Sally Jessy ...ael" show, on which Sally Perdue appeared to talk about ... affair with Governor Bill Clinton.*

**ALLY JESSY RAPHAEL:** Today, another woman who claims she had an affair with democratic presidential candidate Bill Clinton. Does the American public really care about the private lives of politicians? Stay with us.

A couple of days ago I received a fax that read, "Sally Perdue, a former Miss Arkansas and controversial radio and television personality will be appearing in New York to tell her story of her sexual affair with Bill Clinton during his second term as governor." Now, when we received this fax, we were kind of skeptical about it and said to ourselves—first question you'd ask—"Does anybody care what a person does in private if he is a presidential candidate?" And you know what, we've asked some people and I don't know. We went back and forth on this a lot and we made the decision to ask you the question today. Now the catalyst. Joining us is Sally Perdue . . .

**Ms. PERDUE:** I've known Bill or known of Bill, I guess, since 1973. I was from Arkansas. I was very visible, had a television show and worked for a PBS station that was funded by the legislators. So I spent a lot of time in the senate. I worked for the state senate for a while, so I was around all these people. And there was an attraction, I guess, from the very beginning . . . I came back to Arkansas about '83 and—I don't want to get ahead of myself or behind myself but—I moved an engine out of the park to rebuild Pine Bluff's image. I was from Pine Bluff, Arkansas. I had been in New York and I felt really powerful and I felt like if anyone could turn their image around that had just been recently named the second worst city in the United States to live in, that I could do that by restoring this engine. Because I'm a rail buff and

because my father was a 39-year veteran with the
Railroad. I was very proud of my heritage. So this
engine came out of the park and I saw the possib.
not only could it enhance Pine Bluff's image but
enhance the image of the State of Arkansas because
wonderful train memorabilia. And we needed to just g.
legislature to set up a non-profit so that we could have
focus. And that was my reason then for getting to Bill o.
one-to-one basis. I went through the Parks and Tourism, the
wouldn't help, and finally went to Bill.

**SALLY:** When you met him, you said there was an initial—

**Ms. PERDUE:** There was, even in '73. I was thrown with him
at a golf tournament—

**SALLY:** Would you say you were the pursuer or would you say
he was the pursuer?

**Ms. PERDUE:** I think it was a mutual—I think he saw in me
maybe something that was a little different from your Arkansas woman.

**SALLY:** Now, was he married at this time?

**Ms. PERDUE:** When I first met Bill, he was not in '73. But—

**SALLY:** No, when the affair took place?

**Ms. PERDUE:** Yes. And I—I certainly accept full responsibility for that. I was not married. He was married.

**SALLY:** Did it disturb you that this was a married man?

**Ms. PERDUE:** No, it did not disturb me because it was an
affair of the moment. I was not looking beyond that.

**SALLY:** Where did the sexual side of the affair take place?

**Ms. PERDUE:** In my condominium, in Little Rock.

**SALLY:** Did you go to dinner together in public places?

**Ms. PERDUE:** No, we were never seen publicly.

**SALLY:** You were never seen publicly?

**Ms. PERDUE:** There were people in the condominium complex that saw us. I told my friend Anna who is here.

**SALLY:** Yes, sitting next to Sally is Anna Lisenbuy. Anna is,
would you say best friend?

**JE:** Yes. We've know each other since junior high. Anna, you say you knew about Sally's relationship ll Clinton how?

**LISENBUY:** Sally Perdue's Best friend: Just by her g me.

**Y:** By her telling you? did you ever see him at-

**LISENBUY:** NO.

**LLY:** -her condominium?

**Is. LISENBUY:** No.

**SALLY:** Did you ever call when they were there.

**Ms. LISENBUY:** I called over there and Sally says, "I can't talk, he's here." And that, I assume, was, you know.

**SALLY:** How long did the affair go on?

**Ms. PERDUE:** It lasted between three-and-a-half and four months. It was very short-lived.

**SALLY:** Why did it break up?

**Ms. PERDUE:** That's interesting, Sally, because it actually broke up when it got beyond a physical attraction and turned into a mental challenge. I told him that I planned to run for mayor of Pine Bluff. I felt that in order to ensure the future of this engine, to ensure the reason that I planned to move it out, which was to restore Pine Bluff's image, that I needed to be the mayor. And that's when he came down on me pretty hard and said, "You are not a politician. You don't even know the lingo. You can't identify with the democrats or with the republicans. How do you expect to win this race? . . .

**SALLY:** All right, what I'm understanding, Sally is you feel that he dropped you.

**Ms PERDUE:** He didn't drop me. No, we actually had an argument. There was no dropping to it.

**SALLY:** Was the argument the end of the relationship?

**Ms. PERDUE:** Yes, it was. It was, "You'd—You'd better not run for mayor."

**SALLY:** Because he did not want you to run for mayor?

**Ms. PERDUE:** I don't think he really wanted me to be an independent thinker at that point. I think that—

**SALLY:** OK, that's very interesting thing to get to.

**Ms. PERDUE:** and that's really what this is about, S...

**SALLY:** But let me understand something first. Were ... love with him?

**Ms. PERDUE:** No.

**SALLY:** Was he in love with you?

**Ms. PERDUE:** No.

**SALLY:** Did he ever tell you he was in love with you?

**Ms. PERDUE:** No, no, no, no. It was not—I don't even like to call it an affair, it was an encounter.

**SALLY:** Why come forward and talk about this? Why not just keep your own counsel like a million women do?

**Ms. PERDUE:** And I've tried that.

**SALLY:** OK. I understand that you didn't come forward because you felt they were pressuring you. But is there something you feel about the governor?

**Ms. PERDUE:** This is not a session to bash Bill Clinton. I feel of the three candidates running, Bill is probably the most qualified because he spent years grooming for this position . . .

**SALLY:** Will you vote for Bill Clinton?

**Ms. PERDUE:** I will not vote for anyone. After my year as a politician, I became totally disenchanted with the entire political system . . .

**SALLY:** In your opinion, how does Bill Clinton stand on women and their issues?

**Ms. PERDUE:** I think as long as he can manipulate the women and they do as he wishes them to do—

**SALLY:** Well now wait, manipulating women is not what we're about.

**Ms. PERDUE:** You asked me how I felt that Bill Clinton-

**SALLY:** I'm sorry I interrupted. I shouldn't have. Go ahead.

**Ms. PERDUE:** Go ahead. No, no, no, no, you ask me the question again, Sally.

**SALLY:** OK, how do you feel Bill Clinton stands on women's issues, and what does he privately, as a person, think about women in general? What is his attitude toward women?

**Ms. PERDUE:** I really don't know that Bill feels strongly about

's issues. I think that Bill is saying what he thinks
n want to hear.

**Y:** That means he's duplicitous.

**PERDUE:** I would take it to mean that.

**LY:** OK. Did he express attitudes toward women that let
you think he was less than an egalitarian?

**s. PERDUE:** We were in it for the fun and games. And
serious conversation was not to be brought up.

**SALLY:** A woman who is having an affair with a man can tell
pretty much in- There's got to be some conversation, even if
you tore off your clothes as you ran in the apartment. You
can get a feeling if you're dealing with the liberated male of
*M*A*S*H* or a good old boy of the South. And I guess I'm
asking pretty directly. I mean, I'll keep doing it.

**Ms. PERDUE:** He's a product of the good old boy of the South.

**SALLY:** He is?

**Ms. PERDUE:** Yes, very definitely.

**SALLY:** Is the good old boy—

**Ms. PERDUE:** That's why women are threatened. There are
no women in the good old boys' system.

**SALLY:** That's pretty strong—OK, joining the show is Sally's
daughter, were talking about your daughter. This is Myra . . .
What did you think when she told you about the affair?

**MYRA PERDUE SACK,** Sally Perdue's Daughter: Well, I
was not surprised. I had known that they had been friends
for a long time, that they had worked together on different
projects. I knew they had been colleagues of sorts. I had not
made the connection . . .

**SALLY:** Then you're saying you do not feel that your statements will be damaging to Governor Clinton.

**Ms. PERDUE:** No, no not at all.

**SALLY:** You do not?

**Ms. PERDUE:** No. He's—He's well-insulated. And I don't
think that anything I say—And my purpose in coming here,
Sally, is not to do this—The press clip that you got that said
I was coming to tell my story, I could have had a press conference, I didn't.

**SALLY:** Right . . .

**Ms. PERDUE:** I didn't bring it out at this moment, it out in Atlanta . . . And it was, as I said, squelche

**SALLY:** Well, we didn't squelch. In fact, we called the C campaign to see what they had to say about it and they they would not make a formal statement at this time . .

[Questions taken from the audience] . . .

**AUDIENCE MEMBER (#1):** Did it ever occur to you th. while you were having this affair with Bill Clinton that it would ever come out?

**Ms. PERDUE:** No . . . I can only claim that I was very impulsive at the moment. and, as I said—let me—Let me make sure that you understand, I never went into this with the idea I was going to have an affair. It started with one time and then it was another time and then it was another time. And I think any woman that ever has an affair doesn't go into it with the idea, "Well, this thing is going to last a year and I'm going to get him to marry me," or whatever. That was never an issue, no . . .

**AUDIENCE MEMBER (#2):** A question for Sally. If you were the only one that knew about this, no one saw you, your friend never saw you, how did this come out in the first place?

**Ms. PERDUE:** There were four people that knew. One is dead, one is sitting on the stage with me. Two of those people that knew wanted to tell the story until they were approached by someone in Arkansas. I can't say—First of all, I didn't plan to use this, otherwise I would have taken videotapes, I would gave taken photographs, or I would have made sure that someone saw me.

**SALLY:** Or you would have sold it. Question:

**Ms. PERDUE:** I have not sold the story. I don't intend to sell the story. I'm hoping that it will come out one time, I will have my say, and then it will just melt into nothingness.

**SALLY:** Question.

**AUDIENCE MEMBER (#3):** I find you've been very, very inconsistent, in the sense that, on the one hand, you say that you would prefer that it not affect his campaign, and yet you

...hat he's a good old boy from the South, that women ...opportunities in his administration and that his stands ...men's issues is narrow-minded.

...RDUE: If you're willing to accept what I'm telling you ...you still want to vote for him, that's fine. I'm not here ...bash Clinton. I'm telling you the facts. I want to know the ...acts before I vote for anyone.

# APPENDIX G

*Below is a copy of page 300 of the Bill Clinton for P.
Committee's Federal Election Commission July 1992 .
showing payments to private investigator Jack Palladino.*

SCHEDULE BP
Bill Clinton for President Committee
ITEMIZED DISBURSEMENTS
July 1 - July 31, 1992

Page 300 of 451
Line 23

| PAYEE/ADDRESS PURPOSE | DATE | FOR | AMOUNT |
|---|---|---|---|
| Ozaas, Nancy E.<br>4 Fourth Street , SE<br>Washington DC 20003 | | | |
| Salary | 07-18-92 | PRIMARY | 242.87 |
| P.C. Computer Rental<br>460 West 31st 9th Floor<br>New York NY 10001 | | | |
| Furniture/Equipment | 07-14-92 | PRIMARY | 508.00 |
| P.C. Computer Rental<br>460 West 31st - 9th Floor<br>New York NY 10001 | | | |
| Furniture/Equipment | 07-15-92 | PRIMARY | 986.47 |
| P/Ek Press Inc.<br>P.O. Box 235<br>Westfield NJ 07090 | | | |
| Printing/Reproduction | 07-01-92 | PRIMARY | 5,163.05 |
| Pacific American Telephone<br>4329 Ambrose Avenue<br>Los Angeles CA 90027 | | | |
| Telephone Services | 07-09-92 | PRIMARY | 1,000.00 |
| Palladino, Jack<br>1482 Page Street<br>San Francisco CA 94117 | | | |
| Legal Services | 07-01-92 | PRIMARY | 12,824.79 |
| Palladino, Jack<br>1482 Page Street<br>San Francisco CA 94117 | | | |
| Legal Services | 07-24-92 | PRIMARY | 5,003.40 |
| Palladium<br>136 East 14th Street<br>New York NY 10003 | | | |
| Event/Catering Expense | 07-14-92 | PRIMARY | 1,000.00 |

SUBTOTAL of Expenditures this page - 26,728.58

# APPENDIX H

*... a letter from Bill Clinton dated July 1, 1992, in which ...resses his support for abortion and the controversial ...dom of Choice Act," which allows for abortion in all nine ...hs of pregnancy.*

July 1, 1992

Dear ████████:

I believe that personal privacy is a fundamental liberty protected by our Bill of Rights.  The right to privacy includes the right to make difficult and intensely personal decisions regarding abortion, without governmental interference.  <u>I have never wavered in my support of Roe v. Wade.</u>

Over the course of this campaign, <u>I have repeatedly called for national health insurance which would cover the cost of pregnancy-related medical procedures including abortions.</u>  In Arkansas, I have fought against mandatory waiting periods and parental and spousal consent laws.

If elected President, <u>I will sign the Freedom of Choice Act to secure the right to choose in federal law</u> and an Executive Order repealing the "gag" rule, which undermines privacy rights and First Amendment rights of health care providers.

Sincerely,

*Bill Clinton*

# APPENDIX I

*Below is Bill Clinton's September 26, 1986 letter to the A
Right to Life office expressing his opposition to abortion*

STATE OF ARKANSAS
OFFICE OF THE GOVERNOR
State Capitol
Little Rock 72201

September 26, 1986

Arkansas Right To Life
P.O. Box 1697
Little Rock, AR  72203

Dear ▇▇▇▇▇▇▇▇

Thank you for giving me the opportunity to respond to the
Arkansas Right to Life Questionnaire.  However, most of the
questions address federal issues outside the authority of a
governor or the state.

Because many of the questions do concern the issue of
abortion.I would like for your members to be informed of my
position on the state's responsibility in that area.  I am
opposed to abortion and to government funding of abortions.
We should not spend state funds on abortions because so
many people believe abortion is wrong.  I do support the
concept of the proposed Arkansas Constitutional Amendment
65 and agree with its stated purpose.  As I have said, I am
concerned that some questions about the amendment's impact
appear to remain unanswered.

Again, thank you for allowing me to share my position on
this important issue.

Sincerely,

Bill Clinton

Bill Clinton

BC:kt

# APPENDIX J

**777 EAST WISCONSIN AVENUE**
**MILWAUKEE, WISCONSIN 53202-5381**
**TELEPHONE 414-271-0900**
**FACSIMILE 414-271-6134**

March 25, 1992

TO:  ALL MEMBERS OF THE WISCONSIN ACADEMY
     OF TRIAL LAWYERS

     I am writing this letter on behalf of Bill Clinton for
President. It would seem that the tort system is principally under
attack from President Bush and Vice-President Quayle. In short,
their attack on lawyers and the tort system in general is not very
discriminating and that our view as trial lawyers who practice in
the adversary system should take precedence over historical party
affiliation.

     I happen to know that Bill Clinton is against tort reform
of any kind and is a strong friend of the victims of wrongful
conduct. He is, on record, opposing the proposals promoted by
Vice-President Quayle and his Competitiveness Council.

     Accordingly, I urge all of you to write a check to the
Clinton for President campaign and forward it to me so that I can
batch them together and send them on to Little Rock, Arkansas.
Governor Clinton is holding a fundraising reception in Milwaukee
on April 3rd and, if any of you would like to attend the reception,
please contact Cindy at my office for more information.

     It's extremely important that President Bush not be
allowed to further erode the rights of our clients, present and
future. There are many reasons to support Bill Clinton over
President Bush on other issues, but on the one issue that affects
all of us equally there is no choice other than Bill Clinton.
Hoping to hear from you soon, I remain,

           Very truly yours,

           Robert L. Habush

RLH/cac

# APPENDIX K

*Below is David Williams's July 10, 1992 letter soliciting contributions for the Clinton campaign. Mr. Williams is President of the Arkansas Trial Lawyers Association.*

## ARKANSAS TRIAL LAWYERS ASSOCIATION

Office of the President
David M. Williams

Suite 350, Gans Building
217 West Second Street
Little Rock, AR 72201

Telephone: (501) 372-0058
Fax: (501) 376-2347

July 10, 1992

Dear

I have known Bill Clinton since he came to teach at the law school in Fayetteville where I was a student from 1972-1975. It wasn't too long afterwards that Bill Clinton entered his first political race in which he decided to take on the most firmly entrenched, highly Republican John Paul Hammerschmidt, and actually made a respectable race out of it.

After that, he ran successfully for Attorney General and then Governor. There have been a lot of us who have been with him from the beginning; lawyers who were students under the Governor when he was a young professor at the University. During all this time, I can never remember an occasion when he failed to do the right thing where we trial lawyers were concerned.

Just look at our record. Arkansas is one of only four states that has survived the insurance industry's propaganda war unscathed. We have no tort reform/deform here in Arkansas. In addition, we have been very successful in our own legislative efforts. This success would not have occurred without Bill Clinton.

I remember that in 1987 the Governor responded to the nationwide state of alarm over rising insurance rates with a legislative package that had some insurance premium control features to it as well as some tort reform features. The tort reform features would have modified joint and several liability, changed the collateral source rule, and imposed some limitations on punitive damages. We immediately got on the horn to the Governor about this and the tort reform part of the legislative package was buried. I was persuaded that there were some folks on the Governor's staff that had included the tort reform in his legislative package without his approval, and the press somehow got hold of it before the Governor had any real opportunity to sit down and review it. In any event, the Governor dropped the tort reform and it has never come back up.

During another session, I remember a bill that had whistled through
the Arkansas House and Senate that would have given immunity from
liability to "good samaritan" doctors who provided medical care to
indigent patients. This proposed act went to the Governor's desk for
his signature. Once again, we got on the horn to the Governor with
the message that if this proposal became law, it would be tantamount
to telling poor people in Arkansas that they didn't deserve the same
quality of medical care as those folks who could afford to pay for it.
The Governor agreed wholeheartedly and vetoed the bill. I would say
that this act took some strength of character and conviction.
However, this is not unusual. Bill Clinton has always been sensitive
to these kinds of issues.

So, can I recommend that your folks put their money behind Bill Clinton
for President? Not just yes, but hell yes. And without belittling
Bill Clinton's candidacy, I've got to ask, what other choice is there?
How could anybody even think there was another choice. When I look at
the damage that 12 years of Republican rule under Ronald Reagan and
George Bush has done to the Federal Judiciary and the United States
Supreme Court in regard to consumer and environmental issues, and the
whole broad spectrum of human rights that concern us and our clients,
there can be no other choice.

Oh I hear the criticism of Clinton by those folks who call him "Slick
Willy." They say he listens to the polls first and then reacts.
Well, they all react to the polls and they all attempt to curry favor
and win votes where they can. But, in his heart of hearts, Bill
Clinton is guided by that instinctive will to do what's right for the
common man. So dig down deep and give to Bill Clinton. He's the only
choice for us trial lawyers and the little folks we represent.

Sincerely yours,

David H. Williams

DHW/sb